Eternal Scoreboard

Eternal Scoreboard
A Different Way to Win

Tammy Cooper Zimmerman

Published by Game Changer Publishing

Note: Scripture references in this book are drawn from multiple translations of the Bible. In some cases, passages have been paraphrased for clarity, emphasis, or devotional purposes. Emphasis added.

Paperback ISBN: 979-8-90158-140-7
Hardcover ISBN: 979-8-90158-134-6
Digital ISBN: 979-8-90158-135-3

www.GameChangerPublishing.com

To my husband, Mike Zimmerman.
My most valuable blessing gifted from God.

Read This First

Thank you for reading my book! Scan below to access a free, downloadable resource I've created for you.

Scan the QR code here:

Eternal Scoreboard

A Different Way to Win

TAMMY COOPER ZIMMERMAN

Foreword

Climbing the ladder of success in modern American culture can be a brutal and trying journey. Few make it to the top without the shedding of blood, sweat, and tears. However, one thing might be worse than never making it to the top: making it to the top and finding out your ladder is resting against the wrong destination.

A midlife crisis is less about a feeling of failure from not reaching your goals and much more about reaching your goals and discovering that they aren't all they were cracked up to be. The result of this internal angst has led me to believe that the successful often look incredibly complete on the outside but are dying on the inside. First, the pressure they are under is immense. The more successful you are, the more you have to manage and the more personalities you have to lead. Second, the successful are often lonely. In the need to be perceived as strong, there is little room for the vulnerability required for human flourishing. Third, the successful are hungry for meaning more than achievements, affirmation, and affluence. They are spiritual creatures, just like the rest of humanity, who were made for more than the survival of the fittest. They long for meaning in a life that matters and contributes to things that matter.

The Eternal Scoreboard shines bright as a journey that not only sets your ladder on what matters most but also offers wisdom on how to climb it. Tammy's weaving of her personal stories, her business-savvy direction, and the spirituality of the heart makes this book unique and a must-read for any Christian seeking success first in the Kingdom of God, while also glorifying Christ through excellent work in the kingdom of this world. It is also a perfect guide for those who may not share the same spiritual convictions but find themselves longing for more than exhaustion on the treadmill of success.

I've known Tammy and Mike for around two decades. I had the honor of being their pastor for most of those years. Ironically, they sought to bless my life and steward our friendship as much as, or even more than, I did for them. Tammy's story of tenacity, seasoned with a tenderhearted love for people and for God, is inspiring. Her personal stories and the lessons she learned along the way are riveting. They invite the reader into a relationship with her that never talks down to the reader, as many books do. She resists any notion of leaving the reader feeling ashamed or like a failure. Instead, we journey with her through her struggles and strengths, her victories and failures, and more than anything, through her humble spirit that continually seeks to remain teachable.

Having known Tammy for a long time, none of these qualities surprise me. Tammy and Mike live with a radar that seeks out those around them who feel left out, stained, struggling, or inferior. Their radar searches for those who need love, and it comes with the kingdom courage to act on what they see. Tammy is generous with her success in every way possible. She is especially generous with her time and attention to those around her. That generosity is evident on every page of this book.

Even more, *The Eternal Scoreboard* boils down the complexity of success in the modern age into simple, laser-focused wisdom. Her advice is not only strong but also achievable. Nothing is more frustrating than reading advice that cannot be applied to your own setting. Tammy wastes no time in her succinct chapters that get right to the point. She even coaches the reader with clear steps of action. As a communicator, I discovered a long time ago that making the simple complex is easy, but making the complex simple is challenging and can only be achieved by someone who not only understands the concept but has embodied the virtue within it. Tammy's experience in business and in faith places her at the fulcrum of coaching the rest of us with practical and achievable plans of action for anyone who desires to "do all that they do for the glory of God" (1 Cor. 10:31).

I cannot recommend *The Eternal Scoreboard* enough to those who desire wisdom to climb the ladder of success while also making sure their ladder rests on the right destination.

–Dr. Nathan Joyce, Ph.D.
Senior Pastor, Heartland Church
Paducah, KY

Table of Contents

INTRODUCTION

Hello, my name is Tammy Zimmerman. I am an entrepreneur, a businesswoman, a wife, and, most importantly, a child of God.

The purpose of this book is to honor God and share my story. I want to illuminate the simple life I've led, which, while it may not seem spectacular, has been made remarkable by God's influence. He has brought incredible people, opportunities, and a loving husband into my life. This book is intended for anyone who aspires to live a purposeful life.

You should consider taking my advice because my story is authentic and real. I truly believe that the messages contained in this book can help you. My advice has the potential to transform your life, leading you to a richness defined not only by worldly success but also by godly fulfillment.

Within these pages, you will find practical ideas, philosophies, prayers, and techniques designed to enhance your journey, allowing you to navigate life with greater enjoyment, purpose, and, ultimately, success.

My hope is that each chapter provides you with tangible benefits you can readily apply to improve your life. I have added **Practice Sessions** at the end of each chapter to help you navigate applying the ideas in the chapter. I want them to have an impact after reading this book, and I pray they help you. Thank you for joining me on this journey.

PART 1

WHO YOU ARE WHEN NO ONE'S WATCHING

I was six years old when I started piano lessons at my Catholic school with Sister Maria. One of the events we entered was the state piano competition. This was different from a recital because your performance was judged and ranked. These events made my practice sessions much more necessary, intense, and focused.

I wanted with all my heart to do well. I had to learn the piece; I had to get comfortable playing the piece, and I had to memorize the music. These were not things you could do in one day; you had to repeat the piece over and over. I would make mistakes. I would recognize my weak points and focus on them until the kinks were worked out. I would internalize the music so that it came out through my fingers with ease.

A practice session is a scheduled period of time dedicated to rehearsing, training, or improving a specific skill, activity, or performance through repetition and focused effort. These practice sessions never made it to the stage, but they did determine how well I performed.

Faith in God is built in the quiet drills of daily obedience and prayer, not under the stadium lights. Practice sessions require a rich walk with God and represent the private side of faith. This is where you see the hand of

God, prayer habits are formed, godly character is developed, and trust in God is cemented.

Modern culture glorifies "the game" (success, spotlight, recognition) but often overlooks preparation.

Here's a preview of Part I – Who You Are When No One Is Watching:

Chapter 1: Doing a Video Replay

- Finding joy and peace in trusting God with the outcome.

Chapter 2: Know Who You Are

- Uncovering your true identity in Christ.

Chapter 3: When God Is Easy to Miss—Recognizing the Invisible Hand

- Recognizing God's quiet work in your life.

Chapter 4: Self-Talk, Affirmations, and Being Your Best Coach

- Transforming your self-talk through God's truth.

Chapter 5: People Need People

- Remembering that you are not meant to do life alone.

I invite you to treat the next few chapters like a spiritual training camp. Come with a heart to engage. Slow down, reflect, and practice each exercise with intention. This is not meant to be done with perfection but with a heart attached to God's spirit. It is a process done in small steps. It's in the unseen reps of faith that strength is built and transformation happens.

Our Father, who art in heaven, the Creator of the bright stars in the dark sky. Thank You for listening to my prayers. I come before You, asking You to help me see the importance of preparation, humility, and private faithfulness. Let me recognize Your ways and be in touch with Your spirit to let go of the world's ways and grasp the eternal ways. We pray this in the precious name of Jesus. Amen

CHAPTER 1

Doing a Video Replay

"Now all glory to God, who is able, through his mighty power at work within us, to accomplish infinitely more than we might think or ask."
– Ephesians 3:20

I'm a huge sports fan. I love participating in sports, watching games, and reading sports books. I think I've read everything by former professional football coach Tony Dungy. When the Olympics are on, I watch nothing else. In 1996, I was thrilled to be able to go to the Olympics in person.

That year, Atlanta, Georgia, hosted the Summer Olympics. It was a big deal. Businesses actually shut down in anticipation of the large number of people expected to come to the city. I can remember getting a FedEx package ready with a proposal and sweating and scrambling to get it in by noon because everything was going to shut down.

We lived close to the Decatur MARTA station, a great location. We could have rented our house out, but we opted to stay and experience the event, creating memories. We bought tickets and invited my aunt, who is like a sister, and her husband and their young son to come and participate.

You would have thought our house was part of the Olympic Village. We had Team USA Cheerios for breakfast, wore plastic medals at each meal, and dressed in red, white, and blue. We went to events in the heat of the day and the cool of the night. We almost couldn't sleep at night from the excitement. We shouted, "U.S.A.!" so much that our dreams were loud with the same words.

It was during this experience that I recorded my first sporting event. It was a Tuesday night, and the women's gymnastics team, the Magnificent Seven, was going for the team gold medal. We did not have tickets for this, so we taped the event. My husband and I stayed up, but my aunt and her husband were exhausted and went to bed, saying they would watch it the next day.

The team was made up of seven talented, hardworking girls. The event came down to one person and one event. The person was Kerri Strug, an eighteen-year-old from Tucson, Arizona. The event was the vault. One person in a huge arena of red, white, and blue fans. All her hours of training and competitions were for this one moment. The pressure of performing for her team and country. The pressure of the American flag. She must have felt like a boiling water kettle ready to whistle. It was so tense, I had to watch the TV screen with my hands over my face, peeking through my fingers. You would have thought I was watching a scary movie.

Kerri Strug had two chances to clinch the gold. On her first vault, she landed wrong and fell, injuring her right ankle. With all the pressure moved up a notch, she took off running on her second vault and stuck the landing on one foot. Once completed, she collapsed to the mat in agony, and they had to carry her off it.

My husband and I watched all of this, feeling all the colors of red, white, and blue: patriotism, pride, and the love of the team. Once she landed the vault, we were beyond excited. My husband, Mike, told me not to tell my aunt who won but to keep it a secret.

The next morning, she asked if we could watch the video. I knew Mike had told me not to tell her who won, but I asked her if she wanted to know the winner. She said she wanted to know, so I told her. We watched the video, but this time, I knew who'd won. This time, I did not feel like I was watching a scary movie. Instead, I felt like I was watching *The Sound of Music*. I did not have a pit in my stomach. My heart rate had dropped. I was confident and excited.

When Strug fell the first time, I did not feel like it was over. I felt like it was time to fight and win. She did the second vault, landed it, and won. Just like the first time I'd watched, I felt so excited when she won. It was more enjoyable to watch the second time because I knew the outcome. I was more confident and calm.

Watching a taped session, you're excited and enthusiastic. You feel confident and determined. In contrast, when you're watching live, you often feel nervous and anxious, sometimes even panicky. In those moments, fear often overrides the fight within you. The reality of living our life with the assurance that God already knows the final outcome versus living in a reality where you do not have any idea of the outcome creates two very distinct lives.

One year into my marriage with Mike, my boss asked me to move to Boulder, Colorado, to manage an acquisition we had just completed. Mike and I took several walks about our block as I laid out the proposition. On the second lap, we wondered how Mike could leave his successful job after seventeen years. We did not know where we would live, and I had to give my boss an answer the next day. By the fourth lap around the block, after a few prayers in our hearts, we said, "This is the right thing to do, and it is a valid and good risk to take."

We did not make the decision without any idea of the outcome. We felt assured that God was with us. By the fifth lap around, we said, "Let's do this." The next day, I told my boss "yes," and three days later, I moved to Colorado. Mike followed a few months later.

Ephesians 3:20 says, *"Now all glory to God, who is able, through his mighty power at work within us, to accomplish infinitely more than we might think or ask. "* I know that Mike and I would not have been able to make that decision without a mighty power at work. It was a huge risk for us very early in our married life.

This decision of ours paid off not only in worldly success but also in godly success. The godly successes were big and had lasting implications. They are things that money cannot buy. Because it was early in our marriage, we had to create new routines. We learned about each other and the power of two over just one. We grew in faith together. God blessed us with wonderful neighbors: Otto, a Holocaust survivor, and Daisy.

Later in life, because we'd lived in a small town in Colorado, we were able to leave Atlanta and move to a small town in Kentucky. We would never have done that without the experience in Colorado. All of these are godly successes.

I truly believe that if you dedicate your life to God and follow His will, you will discover purpose. When you understand and believe the gospel, you realize that you have already won the battle because of the promise of eternal life in heaven. When you step out of your own perspective and embrace God's plan for you, you receive power and courage, and peace replaces anxiety.

You realize you have someone to rely on, someone who shares wisdom with you and is crafting a plan that is ultimately for your benefit. It may not align with your desires, but it is for your good. When you align the gifts God has given you with His plan, you will experience rich, godly success. You can win this game, too. You can live your life with excitement and confidence, facing challenges head-on.

While you may experience anxiety and fear from time to time, you don't have to let those feelings dominate your life. Ultimately, you want to replace anxiety with peace. The way to do this lies in your belief. Do you believe in God's will? If you don't, it's easy to waver. However, if you genuinely trust in God's will, you will find that your anxiety diminishes. It might not disappear, but it will be less. **When you live like the game's already won, your anxiety begins to lose its power, peace replaces panic, and you manage your fear so there is power in your decisions.**

This inner strength gives you more fight. I've seen too many people give up. They do not fully believe in themselves or, more importantly, in God, which robs them of that fighting spirit.

My greatest blessing is godly success, not worldly success. God blessed me with my husband, Mike. He is truly my best blessing. Our marriage is a priceless gift. I believe that godly success is far more valuable than any worldly achievement.

Through God's influence, I have achieved some worldly success. In fact, much of my story is worldly, but it has been accomplished in a supernatural way. I became the first woman at Global Payment Systems to receive the Corporate Person of the Year award, a title previously awarded only to men. I was also a founding member of Elavon, where our team had the honor of taking the company public on the New York Stock Exchange. I founded Payment Plus Incorporated and sold it to Parthenon Capital. These accomplishments represent worldly successes that I view as opportunities from God.

I share these experiences not to boast, but to highlight what God has done in my life and to give Him glory. When you ask for something, make sure your faith is placed solely in God. *"Do not waver; a person with divided loyalties is as unsettled as a wave in the sea, blown and tossed by the wind" (James 1:6).*

I am not a theologian; I am simply a child of God, a wife, and an entrepreneur. I will share with you the significant events in my life to show examples of struggles and outcomes that have strengthened my relationship with God. Because of my faith, my life has been forever changed, and I pray that your life will be transformed as well.

In the next chapter, we will explore the idea of how peace with God's plan connects you to an identity in Christ.

PRACTICE SESSION

Follow the steps and write about your experience with emotion.

Step 1: Watch a live game this week.
Pay attention to your emotions (e.g., tension, uncertainty, and worry).

Step 2: Then watch a recorded game where you already know the winner.
Notice how calm you feel.

Step 3: Write a short reflection comparing the two experiences.

Step 4: Identify one situation in your life right now that feels uncertain.
Write this statement beneath it: *"God already knows the outcome, and I trust His plan."*

Reflection Prayer: *Our Father who art in heaven, help me trust You with the outcomes I cannot control. Teach me to rest in the assurance that You've already written my victory. We pray this in the precious name of Jesus, Amen.*

CHAPTER 2

Know Who You Are

"I knew you before I formed you in your mother's womb."
– Jeremiah 1:5

For years, I would have described who I am by telling someone where I am from, who my parents were, the people I knew, where I went to school, and where I worked. I did not know my identity well or how to define it.

I felt my first identity crisis when I moved to Atlanta. I did not have family there, just a few friends, and no money in the bank. I had moved out of my state, so sports teams and mascots were different. Everything was different. I went to a women's networking function and felt like the tiniest fish in a very big ocean. All the things that had given me confidence and a sense of security in being connected were gone. The idea of an identity rooted in God's design had not yet developed in my mind. I felt very small and weak during that meeting.

I was born in a small town and into a large family. My mom came from a family of nine, and my dad was from a family of five. As the oldest child, I was the eldest grandchild in my mother's family. Although my dad originally wanted a son, he quickly grew to love being a dad to a daughter. This may be one reason I developed a strong interest in sports.

I had a younger brother who was amazing, and I grew up surrounded by many cousins, with family members living nearby and grandparents actively involved in my life. I watched my aunt Laura thrive in management, and my grandmother played a key role in steering a successful business. My mother took on a leadership role in our family business. I thought it was normal for women to lead. Being the oldest in the family and the oldest grandchild gave me a great sense of responsibility. I felt responsible for my brother and my cousins. I felt their presence and attention.

My parents understood their priorities and excelled at implementing them. Everything they did was for the family, and I grew up during a time when most mothers didn't work outside the home. However, my mother worked extensively, not for individual achievement or to boost her ego but for the sake of our family and the benefits it provided. My dad supported her and helped with the kids, and his involvement was also not about personal glory.

My parents did not put a spotlight on their achievements, but they did put one on their children by loving them well. I felt this love because of the time they invested in us. My parents believed in faith, hard work, and family-first values. It was always about the family, not about themselves.

This background played a major role in shaping my identity and how I perceive and believe in myself. Growing up in this environment gave me a sense of security and responsibility, but I misinterpreted aspects of my identity. I equated responsibility with worthiness and achievement with approval.

Our identity isn't something we create through success or approval; it's something God designed long before we were born. God made us to reflect Him, so He created us in His own image: *"In the image of God He created them; male and female He created them."* (Genesis 1:27)

As my relationship with Jesus has developed, I have had to unlearn some of the lies that formed about my identity. God's truth allowed this to happen. One lie I had to learn not to believe in is that I am unworthy of doing more. It is okay to dream bigger and bolder. You can easily become what your family expects of you, but that may not align with what God truly wants for your life. Therefore, taking the risk to dream more and to dream bigger is about rejecting the misconception.

After establishing my career, I questioned whether I was doing what God wanted me to do as a woman in a leadership position. This doubt popped up because of the new community and the church we were attending. My husband and I had moved back to my hometown of Paducah, Kentucky, from Atlanta. In Atlanta, I had many friends and people who worked in leadership roles, but in Paducah, I was a minority. There were so many people who did not work outside the home. I did not have a tribe of working friends. No one really cared that I was a high achiever.

In Atlanta, I had gained recognition for this and felt more powerful. I had achieved everything I thought I wanted, yet I felt an ache and a missing piece I could not explain. I wondered if I was falling short, in some way, of what God wanted. I was afraid I was disappointing God. I faced that internal conflict for quite some time. I felt lonely, sad, and empty. My parents gave me a foundation, and I built on it to become responsible, successful, and driven.

These difficult moments were private, not lived out in public. I feel quite sure no one knew I was having an identity crisis. This was between God and me. At the time, I was looking to expand my business again and grow into a new building. Through journal writing, prayer, the truth of scripture, and the church, I came to terms with the fact that this is how God made me and that it was perfectly acceptable.

Two main scriptures disrupted this conflict. The first one is Proverbs 31:16–18: *"She goes to inspect a field and buys it; with her earnings she plants a vineyard. She is energetic, strong, and a hard worker. She makes sure her dealings are profitable; her lamp burns late into the night."*

The second is Hebrews 11:39–40: *"All these people earned a good reputation because of their faith, yet none of them received all that God had promised. For God had something better in mind for us, so that they would not reach perfection without us."*

I realized I was fine as I am. I was created in the image of God and was a child of God, a daughter of the King. It was fine to be successful, but that was not the thing that was special. Knowing God, being obedient to Him, and glorifying Him were the important things: living my life to reflect the image of God. In retrospect, what I thought was a lie was really just me understanding my identity.

God can rewrite these lies as truth because He truly meets us in our darkest moments. I believe this happens through people, the Word of God, church communities, and prayer. Sometimes, it can be as simple as someone taking a moment alone to pray or reflect on the scriptures. However, the four components I mention here are much more constructive. Reading the Bible alone can be challenging because it's often confusing and can leave you feeling lost. When you have those additional elements, such as support from others, prayer, and a church community, you create a framework that helps transform your mindset.

As you read, you may come across passages that remind you: *I was created in God's image.* Many of us have been told we are insignificant, but that is not true. With support from others and prayer, you'll find encouragement to move forward and embrace your identity in Christ.

It took a significant, challenging conflict in my life for me to rely on God; this transformation didn't occur without some discomfort. It took more time and searching for me to understand that my identity is being a daughter of the King, designed to reflect God's image. Sometimes, it's not the easy or comfortable experiences that propel us to the next step.

You may be parents who are also helping to develop the identity of your children. Take an inventory of what you are teaching them. Understand your priorities and consider how you are supporting them. Make family your priority over self. Your children may not be able to articulate this concept, but they will certainly feel it.

You might have been raised by people who did not help you develop a healthy and sound identity. It will take work to change this narrative, but you can do it. You do not have to accept or live by the lies that others may have told you.

What we believe about ourselves affects all aspects of our lives: the dreams we dream, the goals we set, the attitude we adopt, and the actions we take each day. It is vitally important for you to identify the lies you are believing and acknowledge the truth of who you are.

The list of lies and truths can be very long, but here are a few:

Lie	**Truth**
I am worthless.	I am a miracle of God.
I can't.	I can.
I have to earn love.	God loves me unconditionally.
My worth depends on my success.	My worth comes from Christ alone.
I don't belong.	I am chosen and known by God.
I have to do everything myself.	God is my strength and helper.

Defining my true identity took years. For you, it might be days, weeks, or months, but continue to journal, rewriting your labels until you can craft a new identity statement based on scripture and beginning with *"I am…"*

One of my favorite characters in the Bible is Joseph. His own brothers sold him into slavery. He was a person who came to understand his identity in Christ. He knew God was in control of his life, which trumped the evil in it. He had the strength because of his beliefs.

In this chapter, we looked at Christ's identity in us. In the next, we will look at recognizing God's hand in our lives.

PRACTICE SESSION

I invite you to use the following steps to craft your identity statement and acknowledge the lies that may be standing in your way:

Step 1: Get a journal.

Step 2: Write down the labels you have carried.
These might be titles, achievements, or mistakes.

Step 3: Take time alone and pray.
Ask God to show you which ones are not from Him. What are the *truths*, and what are the *lies*?

Reflection Prayer: *Our Father who art in heaven, thank You for Your Word, through which we come to know who You are. Help us to obey so we can be a reflection of You in the world. In the precious name of Jesus, Amen.*

CHAPTER 3

When God Is Easy to Miss - Recognizing the Invisible Hand

"You go before me and follow me, and You place your hand of blessing on my head."
– Psalm 139:5

It would be shocking to see a scoreboard showing the point totals for the times I overlooked God and did not recognize His hand and for the times I did recognize His hand in action. It would be humbling and fascinating.

A "God sighting" can be an event. It could be an answered prayer. It could be a conversation. It could be an intuition or a feeling of communication. I am certain I've overlooked some of the ways God has been active in my life.

One example comes from my college days. I took a gymnastics class, which was a fun elective that attracted students from freshmen to seniors.

There was a senior girl in my class whose name I do not remember. I do recall that she was tall and athletic, with blond hair. The conversation happened during the class when we were taking a break. It was a short, unplanned conversation about religion, not a serious debate but more of a friendly discussion. It was the first time in my life that I was living without my family, and I had some serious bouts with homesickness. The conversation was encouraging to me, so encouraging, in fact, that when she told me to buy a Harper Study Bible, I figured out a way to get one.

There was no internet, and Amazon deliveries were a science fiction idea. I didn't have a car, but I managed to get a ride to the bookstore that sold this Bible, and I purchased it. I had to work hard to get the Bible, and it had a great impact on my life. I still have that Bible today; it was my first attempt at diving deeper into scripture. I would read this Bible along with the devotional my dad sent me, *The Upper Room*. It helped me with my homesick moments. I didn't know it then, but God was placing a seed in my life that would anchor my faith for decades.

I wish I could thank that girl for her monumental impact on my life, but I can't because I don't even know her name. I almost missed the significance of that moment. Most of God's greatest works in our lives don't come with a spotlight; they come quietly.

As I think about the God-sighting scoreboard again, I realize that it is worth taking inventory of the reasons I miss Him. If I take an inventory of these distractions, I can try not to repeat this pattern. I want to have more points for God sightings on the scoreboard. There are definitely seasons of life and factors that make it more difficult to see them.

One of the main reasons for missing God is busyness. The world today is active and fast-paced. Our activities can distract us from seeing and hearing God, activities that feed our ego and inflate our sense of importance. Being busy can also lead to fatigue. When we are exhausted, it's harder to be aware of God's presence.

The people we surround ourselves with will influence our awareness. If our friend group is focused on self-interest or distracted by social media, it can diminish our ability to recognize God's presence around us. In a culture that promotes self-centeredness, it's challenging to make space for anything else, including spiritual awareness.

Additionally, our phones often contribute to this distraction. For example, today, while I was waiting to pick up my husband from the eye doctor, I found myself mindlessly scrolling through my phone. Realizing I was wasting time, I decided to read an article from *Desiring God* rather than browsing endless social media posts about dresses. Engaging with something meaningful helped me refocus and become more aware of what truly matters.

You can see God by forward awareness and see Him in real time. Or you can see God by looking back in hindsight. You look back and see God's fingerprints. As you take this inventory, you create an inventory of faithfulness, which becomes spiritual fuel for growth and for times of fear and doubt. My story of the Bible and the girl was about seeing God through hindsight.

By taking the posture of forward awareness, you wake up expecting God to move. You walk into events and places with intentionality. You train your eyes to see small moments. You alter your expectations.

You will use both of these forms of spiritual awareness. There is so much comfort in using hindsight to realize that God has your back. You feel loved and not forgotten. Inventory this and use it in the future. Having a forward awareness changes your attitude and confidence in a situation. That forward awareness opens your eyes and attracts blessings. Both activities are healthy for your spiritual growth and aid in your spiritual maturity. As your spiritual maturity increases, hindsight becomes more relevant, and you see God's action more clearly.

Taking time to look back and reflect allows me to create an inventory of the ways God has been present in my life, what He has done for me, what He has promised me, and how He has come through for me on His promises. During moments of vulnerability, when I face fears or uncertainties, I return to this inventory. I remind myself of all the times I have seen His faithfulness: *Why do I doubt now? I've experienced this, and this, and this. Why allow doubt to creep in?* Reviewing that inventory gives me strength and reassurance, keeping me grounded in the truth.

By looking ahead, you prepare for an event. You are alert and receptive to opportunities. Be intentional with that awareness. If you recognize that opportunities for divine experiences can occur, you'll be more likely to notice them. For example, when you step outside to visit the grocery store, meet a friend for coffee, or go to work, being aware and intentional will make you more receptive to conversations, gatherings, or events that may be significant God sightings. If you approach these outings with awareness and intention, you'll be less likely to overlook them. I have missed many of them because, honestly, no one had ever shared this perspective with me before.

There are tangible activities that help us get into God's presence and silence the noise. To feel a stronger connection with God, it's important to dedicate time to building a relationship with the church. Attending church in person, rather than just watching online, allows you to develop meaningful relationships with others. Making the effort to attend church in person can help set a positive tone for your week, starting your Monday on the right foot.

PRACTICE SESSION

Use these strategies to meditate on the Lord.

Step 1: Be quiet with God.
Try setting a two-minute timer on your phone and spend that time in silence. While two minutes might feel long at first, you can gradually extend it to four minutes and eventually work your way up to ten minutes of quiet reflection centered on God.

Step 2: Try exercising outdoors and spending time in nature.
Being in a natural setting feels much more spiritually fulfilling than being surrounded by the hustle and bustle of city life, with all the asphalt, heat, and noise. Taking a walk or going for a hike can help you feel more grounded and connected to God's presence.

Step 3: Start small.
You don't have to take big steps; just take small ones. When you start small, you'll get a sense of what that feels like. This will give you some experience to build upon as you grow.

Step 4: Think back on a moment when something small changed your life.
Could that have been God's hand? Where have you overlooked God because you expect Him to speak loudly instead of quietly?

Step 5: Record these ideas to keep a God-sighting journal for seven days:

Ask yourself these questions each day and write down the answers:

> *Where did I see God in big and small ways today?*
> *What prayer did He answer?*

What whisper or feeling in my conscience do I think was from God?
What movement encouraged me unexpectedly?
What convenience could have been tied to God and not to chance?
What conversation was fueled by God?

Step 6: Take time at the end of the week to pray and connect the dots.

Identify where you can see God in action. You might consider doing this once a month. Practice makes perfect. By doing this regularly, you will become more aware and connect the God dots faster.

Reflection Prayer: *Our Father who art in heaven, let me have the desire to live in the spirit so that, no matter if moving slow or moving fast, I do not miss God sightings or I do not miss the hand of God. In the precious name of Jesus, Amen.*

CHAPTER 4
Self-Talk, Affirmations, and Being Your Best Coach

"Make the most of every opportunity in these evil days."
– Ephesians 5:16

Your belief system determines your boldness, and God-centered affirmation can completely rewire it. This rewiring means change: to make something radically different, to transform it, or to give it a new position, course, or direction. True transformation leaves a lasting impact, much like dyeing a hard-boiled egg; making it naturally white again is next to impossible. This happened to me in an unlikely place.

My first job after college was at a bank, where I attended a professional development seminar called "Stand Up, Speak Out." This event focused on how to give powerful presentations. It took place before the era of PowerPoint, so we relied on handouts and slides. While the technology may have changed, the content was invaluable.

One of the items we received was a cassette tape titled "Affirmations for Achievement." At that time, cassette tapes were commonly used in cars or with standalone players. This tape contained about forty-five affirmations, statements, or beliefs we were encouraged to say out loud over a period of thirty days. These affirmations ranged from goals to expressing love for others.

I committed to this practice, often repeating the affirmations more than once a day, and I continued with it for thirty days, perhaps even stretching it to sixty.

Among all the affirmations, the fourth one was the one that truly changed my life. The way you talk to yourself shapes the way you live, and only God's truth can transform your inner voice. It stated, "You are a miracle created by God." Each day, I reminded myself of this idea: that I was indeed a miracle made by God.

I would listen to the tape in my car, day after day. Hearing that I was a miracle made by God would unlock my heart every time. As I drove, I would listen and think, *Could this be true?* For twenty days, I questioned the truth of this statement. I would banter back and forth with God: *Really, me? A miracle?*

After twenty days, I started to align my heart with this belief, and instead of asking a question, I would state it as a truth: "I am a miracle created by God." I started to believe this truth in my heart, and it made me happy. This realization transformed my identity.

A miracle is something extraordinary, a wonder, a marvel, with God as its creator. Embracing this perspective gave me a solid foundation for a meaningful purpose in life. This foundation began to erode the lie that I could only do a little, not a lot. I began to dream bigger. It deactivated my fear of doing life alone and instilled a confidence that prompted me to take risks.

This new belief system allowed me to dream and decide that I could move and get a better job. Had I not made this shift in my belief system, I might never have dared to dream or achieve anything significant. You have the power to change and control what you believe. Seek the truth; make certain the message you accept is genuine. The Bible serves as a foundational source of truth for many.

My transformation was real because it was God-centered. There is a difference between self-help affirmations and God-centered affirmations. In self-help affirmation, change happens with willpower. The change can be motivational but not transformational. Self-help can become self-focused. God-centered affirmation is based on truth. It is rooted in scripture. It is empowered by the Holy Spirit. It actually reshapes identity, not just mood.

You can stand on God's affirmations and believe statements that reflect the truth. They are

genuine and strong. They are not fake or fraudulent. They serve as a foundational pillar that supports more than just material thinking, like money, career, cars, and homes. These worldly pursuits can be fleeting. They are similar to sugar in comparison to a nutritious meal. They don't provide lasting satisfaction.

If something is truly from God, it resonates deeply. It's like when you watch a sunrise or sunset: so many people see the beauty and think, *Wow, that's beautiful.* Who can look at a rainbow and not be amazed by its beauty? It's incredible! How does it even happen? It's real.

The same goes for your belief in yourself as a miracle. Those truths, which come from God, are genuine and unshakeable. They will never waver. This experience changed my entire belief system. If I hadn't come to see myself as a miracle, I don't think I would have had the courage to take risks and pursue my goals. Which belief about yourself has held you back the most?

Knowing this is real changes how you approach your career goals and relationships. It impacts you by instilling confidence and fostering the ability to dream. This belief encourages you to trust in what God has created. When you have faith in this, you feel blessed, which, I believe, is where you start to find the fight in yourself. It empowers you to continue pushing forward. Have you ever considered which of your current affirmations are rooted in fear or in truth?

Some of the most important conversations you can have are the ones you have with yourself. Be mindful of what you read, what you watch on TV, and how you engage with social media. Protect your heart.

The result is that you become willing to take risks in various aspects of life, whether that's pursuing a new job, making new friends, building relationships, or even getting married. Taking risks involves the possibility of facing rejection or hearing "no." However, once you recognize and embrace the idea that you are a miracle created by God, your resolve strengthens, allowing you to persevere.

In my newfound identity, I was able to craft dreams and goals. I was able to dream bigger. I decided to move to a larger city. I made a list of the top cities and decided on Atlanta. I did not have friends, family, or any business connections there. I made the decisions because I felt there were multiple opportunities for well-paying jobs.

Once I made that decision, I started to work on networking and a plan to get there. I took my vacation that year and went to Atlanta by myself. There, I set up appointments with businesspeople and gathered information. This was an information-gathering trip, not a series of real interviews. I made connections with people when I learned that they lived in Atlanta. I would cold-call them and set up an appointment. Not everyone would meet with me. I got many "no's," but that did not stop me. This new identity gave me risk-taking qualities but also a resilience to rejection, so I would not quit.

When you encounter rejection, instead of deflating, you develop resilience. You bounce back and might think, *I'll try again*, whether that's asking someone to be your friend or pursuing a career opportunity. When faced with a "no," you learn not to take it personally and continue moving forward with determination. What are the sentences you say to yourself most often? Which are beneficial? Which are hurtful?

I was able to schedule some productive meetings. In your career, you might choose a particular path or create something new. You weigh the risks, recognizing that sometimes things will work out and sometimes they won't. If you truly believe you are a miracle of God, it helps shape your thought process. You won't make hasty decisions; instead, you'll seek logical outcomes, whether in your career or in relationships with the right people.

It can be intimidating to take risks. Many people avoid them and end up stagnating, lacking confidence and self-esteem, because they are too afraid to try anything. That is why it's important to have a strong foundation when taking risks. You may face rejection, but being resilient helps you bounce back from setbacks.

It's crucial to understand that taking risks is a part of life. Sure, you might fail at times, but what's essential is the ability to keep trying. It's perfectly okay to make mistakes; everyone does at some point. What matters is perseverance and the willingness to try again. I believe that God and the Holy Spirit guide you in making the right decisions. Having faith gives you the courage to take risks, even though it can be daunting.

Imagine if every person could truly believe that they are a miracle created by the one true God. It would change the world.

I got lucky, and this affirmation popped up on a tape that was given to me. The odds of this happening for you are slim, so in the Practice Session you can design and create God-centered affirmations. As stated a bit earlier, God-centered affirmations are based on truth. They are rooted in scripture and empowered by the Holy Spirit. They actually reshape identity, not just mood. The focus is on God, not yourself.

Years later, I managed to track down the person who gave that presentation for me, finding her on LinkedIn. We talked on the phone, and I had the chance to tell her what a difference she'd made in my life. It was really great to express my gratitude. Unlike the girl who encouraged me to buy the Bible, I was able to go back and thank this woman.

Communication and people are important, and we are so much like sheep. I'm very grateful I was able to communicate with the person who created the affirmation tape. We need people. That is what we'll cover in the next chapter: people need people.

PRACTICE SESSION

Create your own affirmations or use the following **four powerful, God-centered affirmations.**

1. The same Spirit who raised Jesus from the dead lives in me and gives life to my mortal body. (Romans 8:11)
2. God is my Father, and His perfect love casts out all fear from my heart. (1 John 4:18)
3. I am forgiven, redeemed, and made completely new in Christ. (Colossians 1:14; 2 Corinthians 5:17)
4. I am a miracle created by God. (Psalm 139:14)

Step 1: Tape your affirmations on a recorder or on your phone.

Step 2: Listen to them every day for thirty days.

Step 3: Once a week, journal your thoughts.
What questions do you have? What do you struggle with? What brings joy to your heart? If you have a trusted spiritual mentor, talk to them and get their insight.

Reflection Prayer: *Our Father who art in heaven, I am grateful that You are my ultimate life coach. Let me have the courage to rely on You and only You so that my identity is fastened to Your power, majesty, and love. In the precious name of Jesus, Amen.*

CHAPTER 5
People Need People

"Two people are better off than one, for they can help each other succeed. If one person falls, the other can reach out and help. But someone who falls alone is in real trouble."
– Ecclesiastes 4:9–10

I was fiercely independent in my early years. At church, I wanted to sit by myself, closer to the front. My mom would sit closer to the back with my brother. I wanted that feeling of being on my own or standing by myself. My mom did not allow this very often, but from time to time, she did. I think she thought I would become afraid and return to the back, to her.

I learned early that I could rely on myself, and I enjoyed the experience. It took me several years to realize that independence without community becomes isolation. While this strength has served me well, it has also caused me difficulties.

In high school, I worked at a lovely women's dress shop alongside a great friend. We had such a fun time together. There was this adorable outfit I really wanted, a skirt and top with a peasant look that was in style during the '70s. Unfortunately, I didn't have the money to buy it at the time. My kind mom offered to buy it for me, but I refused. I insisted that she shouldn't do that because it would make me soft.

I have often wondered what motivated a teenage girl to reject a cute outfit. Why? I wanted the glory of doing it myself. It was an achievement for me to buy the outfit myself. All of this was rooted in pride. I believed that if I gave in to this gift, it would erode my power to achieve. That was more important to me than the cute outfit.

I believe that spoiling children doesn't make them better; it makes them weaker. In the end, I never got the outfit, but this experience marked the beginning of my journey to become strong. I was training myself. However, in my race to be independent, I learned that I needed wisdom to recognize that I required people in my life to help me, and I needed God.

It took some challenging lessons for me to fully grasp this truth. During a particularly difficult period in my life, I found myself living paycheck to paycheck and struggling to pay bills. I had recently gone through a traumatic divorce and was feeling very alone as I moved into a new apartment, purchasing the basics I needed.

I did not live close to my parents, so they came to visit me for the weekend. I lived in a small, one-bedroom apartment. You walked in the front door, climbed the dark stairs, and my apartment was on the left. I had a neighbor across the hall. I needed curtains for a sliding-glass door and bedding.

We went to JCPenney, but I soon ran out of money. I had to put a twenty-dollar, blue cotton blanket back on the shelf. I was hurt and disappointed about that. My dad insisted on buying it for me, which led to an argument right there in the store. He said he would buy the blanket, and I insisted he would not.

He then told me that while it's great to be responsible and driven, people need people. We need each other, and sometimes, we need a helping hand. My dad spoke with authority. He knew he was right. He did not just buy the blanket; he also told me why I needed to let someone help me. The "why" is what made the difference.

When I brought it home and put it on the bed, I was glad I'd lost the argument. I was glad my dad had told me why, and I was thankful he cared enough to help me, not just with an object but with his words. I still have that tattered blue blanket to this day.

I learned that day in JCPenney that I needed people. Just like sheep, we are not meant to be alone. I raised sheep, and sheep cannot live alone; they lose their minds. We are built for relationships. It is essential to choose the right relationships, not destructive ones. *"Do not be deceived: 'Bad company corrupts good morals.'"* (1 Corinthians 15:33)

I met Laura the first night of my first MBA class. What a treasure she was then and still is today. We discovered we were in the same industry and, actually, were competitors. We worked in the same area. We helped each other through class and started having lunch together, and I was in her wedding when she got married. We are still friends today. She helped me and made me a better person. Be careful about who your friends are, as they significantly influence your behavior. Godly friends are one of life's sweetest blessings.

It is important to take stock of people's lives: what they do, what they say, and how they live. By observing the byproducts of a person's choices and actions, you can determine whether they will enrich your life or drain it. It's essential to surround yourself with people who bring positivity and enrichment, so conduct this personal inventory thoughtfully. Mentorship, friendship, and building relationships with a church family are all ways to develop the relationships needed.

A key point to remember is not to be afraid of being alone during this process. You don't have to rush into every relationship; it's perfectly fine to spend time alone while you search for the right network of people. Sometimes, being alone serves a purpose, especially if you've just moved to a new town and haven't yet made friends.

If you're in a leadership position, I can promise you, it will feel lonely. You can be surrounded by people but still feel alone. One of the loneliest moments in my leadership journey was when I moved to Colorado to manage an operation we had acquired. My husband did not come for two months. I lived in a Residence Inn. I did not have work friends or personal friends.

The work environment was chaotic after the acquisition. Two cultures had merged, and everyone felt very vulnerable. I retained my position in Atlanta, and this was an extra position, heading up this operations center. I had a very steep learning curve and a heavy workload. I was making decisions about the company and people's lives. It was not just transactional; it was emotional.

A byproduct of the leadership journey is long workweeks. You put time into your venture, which takes away from time with friends and family. I traveled for work, and much of it was alone. I can remember walking through the halls of a hotel, and I would pretend that I was holding the hand of Jesus. This made me not feel so alone. Because of the long hours, I had to say "no" to fun trips and travel with friends and family.

I found support through prayer. I traveled with a small Bible that fit in my briefcase. I felt more secure because it was with me. I had good friends who did not forget about me, even though I was away due to travel. When I returned, they included me. I had some strong professional friends who understood the process and were there to support me.

I had a few godly work buddies. When I was really exhausted or stressed, I would call Paul, our chief technology officer, and he would tell me to look to the mountains God had created. This little moment helped me muster some strength, and I would keep going. It is important to create a network of individuals who can provide support. A small, intimate group of people whom you trust who can help nourish, support, and sustain you. Eventually, my husband came to Colorado, and I had the support of my family.

PRACTICE SESSION

I encourage you to pray about who belongs in your inner circle.

Step 1: Create a list of current relationships.
Write down the people who are currently closest to you or who regularly influence your life. This helps you clearly see who is already part of your inner circle.

Step 2: Reflect on the dynamics of these relationships.
Think about how these relationships affect you—whether they encourage your growth, strengthen your faith, and support your purpose.

Step 3: Pray for God to bring other rich relationships into your life. Be open to this.
Ask God to guide you toward people who will challenge, encourage, and walk alongside you in healthy and meaningful ways.

Next, think about relationships that are misaligned and remove yourself from these draining arrangements. Then think about giving back. Who are you pouring into? How are you helping them? How are you praying for them? People are like sheep; we need each other.

Reflection Prayer: *Our Father who art in heaven, let me come to understand that I am more with others. I need others to be all that You want me to be. I am grateful to be one of Your sheep. In the precious name of Jesus, Amen.*

PART II

THE BIG GAME: STAYING TRUE WHEN THE WORLD PULLS HARD

I never liked practicing the piano, but I did love the competition and performance. The pressure made me focus, and the nerves created energy. I remember feeling like I had a knotted ball in my stomach while waiting for my name to be called before a recital. I felt intense pressure when performing, but also positive excitement that matched the pressure. This was where practice and theory came together in real life. This was where the game was played.

Part II is about the Big Game of Life and how the world will test your values. This is real life. The world will seduce you with fear, money, ambition, rejection, and pressure. Storms, setbacks, and opportunities reveal what you truly believe. Abundance and power are sly ways we are tested. God uses challenges and pressure to deepen character and strengthen spiritual roots. Staying true to His beliefs takes discipline, discernment, and courage. God's voice and coaching become clearer when life gets harder.

Here is a preview of Part II – The Big Game: Staying True When the World Pulls Hard:

Chapter 6: When "No" Is the Real Win

- How God uses rejection and setbacks as redirection.
- Learning to surrender outcomes.
- Seeing "no" as a spiritual win instead of a personal failure.

Chapter 7: Plan It Like It Matters

- Dreaming, planning, and creating with intention while still surrendering to God's direction.
- Holding plans with an "open hand."
- Developing a Kingdom-minded vision instead of a worldly one.

Chapter 8: Money, Money, Money, but Steward It

- The tension between financial success and spiritual obedience.
- Learning to treat money as a tool, not a master.
- Understanding stewardship, ownership, and generosity.

Chapter 9: Lead with Love, Not Power

- How leadership looks when shaped by Christ instead of ego.
- Using influence to lift others, not elevate self.
- How love produces long-term fruit that power alone cannot.

Part I was about identity: *Who you are.*

Part II is about integrity: *How you live and what you believe.*

Life is hard for all of us, and everyone has a story to tell. God is not selective; He created all of us and loves all of us. God is not absent in hardship. Our faith gives us the strength to have the courage to move forward. This faith is not delicate; it is tough and can endure. You can be faithful even when life feels unfair, confusing, or overwhelming.

I invite you to read the next chapters, where I share my real-life stories: the good, the bad, and some ugly.

CHAPTER 6

When "No" Is the Real Win

"Seek the kingdom of God above all else and live righteously, and He will give you everything you need."
– Matthew 6:33

It was a phone call that changed everything for me. I did not get the answer I wanted from this phone call, but I did get a transformed life. Conflict is an area that most people tend to avoid, but the silver lining of conflict is that it fosters personal growth.

In my late twenties, I found myself in a situation I never anticipated: I went through a difficult and surprising divorce. At that time, I was living in a town without any family support and struggling to make ends meet. I made the decision to move to a larger city to find a better job that would allow me to support myself and improve my circumstances.

Every Thursday night, I set aside time to search for a new job and a new city. During this process, one of my customers offered me a position at their well-known company in Louisville, Kentucky, which sold high-end office furniture. Although I was excited about the opportunity, I turned it down because I had plans to move to a larger city with more opportunities. I didn't think it would be fair to accept the job and then leave after just nine months. They appreciated my honesty and connected me with the corporate office in Michigan.

Over the next several months, I had interviews at their corporate office in Michigan and in Atlanta, where their Southeast Division was located. Eventually, I received an offer for a job in Atlanta selling to financial institutions. I was over the moon. I had worked every Thursday night for almost two years, over eighty days. I'd spent three months interviewing in Michigan and Atlanta, seven interviews in all. After all this hard work, it seemed like I had finally reached my goal.

I gave my two-week notice and began planning my move. That's when the conflict arose. I received a call from the corporate office with unsettling news: there was an issue with my job offer, and it might fall through. They wanted to give me a heads-up and promised to call the next day with a final decision.

I had planned, crafted strategies, built relationships, and set realistic goals. I had exhausted every possible route to find the right job, and I was emotionally and physically drained. That night, as I lay in my bed with the blue blanket in my tiny apartment, I felt frightened and alone, with no answers about where to turn. I felt trapped. I had run out of answers.

I prayed to God, expressing my sorrow, repentance, and desire to surrender my life into His hands. I knew that even with all my well-planned efforts, my way of living was not working. I decided that night to live a different life, and it would be God's way. I resolved to live according to His will moving forward. My own efforts were not yielding good results.

I spent most of the night reading the book of Psalms. At that time, I didn't fully grasp all the theological concepts, but something supernatural occurred that night. I did not understand all the implications, but I did understand: *"But when I am afraid, I will put my trust in you" (Psalm 56.3).* This verse, and many more I read that night, fortified me. God heard my prayer and forgave my sins. That night, I began a new journey with Jesus.

The following day, I received a call from the corporate office: I did not get the job. However, I was a different person that day. I meant what I had told God; I was committed to following Him. I made the bold decision to move to Atlanta, knowing that I had no job and limited finances. Exactly one week later, I relocated.

The big pivot move here was understanding that a "no" can actually be a win. We reframe it into an opportunity. When we do not get the answer we want, that does not mean we've hit a dead end. It could be God's redirection, not a rejection. That phone call created significant conflict for me, but it also brought about transformation. Joy can be on the other side of the struggle. Suffering yields character, endurance, and finally hope.

When I arrived in Atlanta, I was not bitter or fearful; instead, I felt positive and optimistic. It was akin to the emotions one experiences while watching a video replay of a game when your team has won. The Holy Spirit was with me, and I knew this was a consequence of my relationship with Jesus Christ and my new prayer life. The Holy Spirit was active in my life.

The company that reneged on its job offer was concerned about my situation and put me in touch with Jack Ritchie, their corporate recruiter in Atlanta. We became friends, and he helped me find a job in an industry that I despised. I disliked the job because of the process you needed to go through to complete a sale. It involved very precise measurements and plans. It was while working at that job, which I hated, that I was offered a job at National Data Corporation.

God was redirecting the "no" into a very positive win. How unlikely it felt that a job I hated would be a bridge to my calling. In a strange way, with some bumps along the road, I ended up in the career I was meant to be in. If I had given up at any point, settled for the status quo, or simply stopped trying, I wouldn't have reached where I believe I was meant to go. It seems I needed to struggle through those experiences to reach the place I needed to be and achieve the success I ultimately found.

It wasn't an easy journey, and it definitely wasn't instantaneous; it took time. However, I didn't give up. I think my prayer and positive attitude were key to my perseverance. I wasn't bitter or fearful, which allowed me to keep pushing forward until I realized I had found my true calling.

I didn't simply buy my confidence off the sale rack; I earned it. I cherish that because I fought through the challenges and refused to give up. I believe many people give up too easily.

I landed at National Data Corporation, now known as Global Payments. It was truly all due to God's guidance, and I am forever grateful. I genuinely appreciate the conflicts and hardships I encountered along the way. These experiences pushed me into a corner, where I made the decision to rely on God. This conflict not only facilitated my growth but also led to a real transformation.

Do not be afraid of suffering or facing seemingly insurmountable challenges. Embrace them with prayer, the Word of God, and the guidance of the Holy Spirit.

What does it look like to reframe a "no" into a win? Define, discern, decide, and do.

Step 1: Define Your Goal

Compare the original goal to the new one: *What did I think I wanted? What might God be shifting me toward?.*

Step 2: Name Your Fears

Identifying what you're afraid of is key. When you receive a "no," panic can set in. By defining your fears, you can move toward that goal, whether it's another relationship, a phone call, or another action item. When you define the fear, you start to break it down, and the power the fear has over you is eliminated. It's like a balloon losing air.

I feared not having money to support myself. Money for my car, rent, and food—just the basics. I had a fear of failure. Once I acknowledged these fears, I could pray, adjust my attitude, write down all the possible failures that could happen, journal ideas, and apply gratitude. Each of these activities keeps us out of the panic syndrome of going nowhere. These activities break the power of fear.

I couldn't have moved to Atlanta with no job and no friends without overcoming my fears. God's help was the most important to me. I do think I was a different person. I believe Jesus faced His fears, and in doing so, He helped me confront mine. Instead of taking my fears away, He empowered me to face them. He gave me courage and humility, qualities I didn't even realize I needed at the time.

I now see that He was obedient to His Father, and in turn, I was being obedient to Jesus without even knowing it. I was different from the inside out. God replaced some of my human flesh with the spirit of Christ, of Him being courageous.

Step 3: Evaluate Your Options

Outline your options by writing them down. Then evaluate the risks and rewards.

Step 4: Set a Date and Take Action

Set dates for your decisions. Write these dates down. Obeying the calendar helps you handle emotional decisions.

People get stuck in the mud and don't go anywhere. They become overwhelmed by their feelings of hurt or rejection. It's important not to take those feelings personally. Taking things personally can keep people stuck because they start to think, *Oh, my gosh, I am a failure; I'm never going to be able to do something different.*

When I made the decision to live life according to God's way and His will, something I didn't fully understand at the time, I truly believed it with all my heart. It felt as if I were saying, *I'm not going down this path; I'm choosing a different one.* I committed to this new route, no matter what. It was as if the decisions were no longer entirely in my control. From that point on, it felt like I had a little guiding presence helping me along the way.

I think He also infused me with a certain energy, a kind of strength that allowed me to navigate my challenges. Jesus definitely possesses that strength, and I believe He shared it with me.

I believe that the qualities I admire in Jesus are also qualities He shared with me. As a human, I still make mistakes, but I feel that love is a central theme in my experience. I think He loves me, which may explain why I didn't harbor bitterness when I moved to my new town; in fact, I really enjoyed it.

Receiving a "no" to the job in Atlanta moved me from pure career thinking to calling thinking. I started out looking for a new job that would pay my bills. I was focused on a career versus a calling. A career is primarily a means to an end, a structured path of jobs for practical reasons, like income, status, stability, or skill building. A calling, in contrast, is a deep internal pull: work that feels purposeful and aligned with your core values, talent, and sense of meaning. It's less about what you do and more about who you are.

I'm not particularly proud of this, but I needed money; it was a basic, instinctual need. I was trying to take care of myself so I wouldn't have to go back home and rely on someone else. My goals and choices were motivated by a career, not a calling. God intervened in the process and blended the two. My career became a calling.

God guided me toward the right calling for my skills and interests. My focus was primarily on improving my financial situation, which might sound cliché or even superficial. I truly believe that God answered my prayers. He provided me with an opportunity that matched my gifts, especially since my brain works well in a technology-driven environment. I came to understand that the new job was a gift from God, and I felt a responsibility to do it well. I felt a partnership with God.

You can see from my story that it's real; He really directs our steps. There might be bumps along the way, like when I took a job that wasn't right for me. However, I truly believe that He will work everything out for our good, as stated in Romans 8:28. *"And we know that God causes everything to work together for the good of those who love God and are called according to his purpose for them."* Is what you are pursuing right now a career, a calling, or something God may be trying to shift?

I believe that's where people tend to give up. They stop along the way and quit rather than continue their journey. Ultimately, you have to trust that God will take care of it all. Every one of us carries at least one "no" that still stings. I invite you to view it through a different lens. Look at the "no" through the lens with God.

PRACTICE SESSION

In this practice session, you will work on making a big pivot. You will walk through a situation that helps you understand that a "no" can actually be a win. The goal is to learn how to reframe a "no" into a new opportunity.

When we don't receive the answer we hoped for, it doesn't mean we should stop. Instead, it may be an invitation to adjust our direction and keep moving forward.

Sometimes what feels like rejection is actually God's redirection.

Step 1: Choose a "no."
Think about a recent or painful "no." It could be a job, a presentation, a project, an opportunity, or a relationship.

Step 2: Write out the story with God in it.
Be detailed, prayerful, and creative. What were you afraid of? Where might God have been protecting or redirecting you? Is there something you see now that you couldn't see then?

Step 3: Ask God for a new goal and first stop.
Pray, *Lord, show me how You want to use this "no" as a new beginning.* Next, write one concrete action you can take this week. At the end of the week, evaluate where you are.

Reflective Prayer: *Our Father who art in heaven, hallowed be Thy name. Thy kingdom come, Thy will be done. Amen.*

CHAPTER 7
Plan It Like It Matters

"You can make many plans, but the Lord's purpose will prevail."
– Proverbs 19:21

I wrote my first goals down forty-two years ago. They were short and sweet. On the top half of the paper were one year's goals. On the bottom half were the next year's goals. I've kept these goals for over four decades. I saved them because this piece of paper is important to me. By writing down my goals, I made my thoughts and dreams real and accountable. This process gave my thoughts and dreams power.

You cannot manage something if you can't measure it. With goals, you can measure your progress. One of the most exciting things I see when reviewing my forty-two years of goals is the difference in them when God became number one in my life. They start to mention Him, and His importance is elevated.

You are the artist of your life. You have a blank canvas before you. You can dream, plan, and create what you want your life to be. The purpose is the fuel, but the plan is the map. Planning matters because it aligns our actions with God's purpose instead of us drifting through life on autopilot.

Early in my career, I began keeping a paper folder filled with a variety of documents, including annual goals, motivational notes, cards, and speeches. This folder gave me a place to fuel my ambition and manage my fears. By year three of writing goals, I no longer jotted down just a list of items, but also included an opening paragraph. My opening paragraph in 1986: *"Enjoy life, but remember that every day is not a vacation. Always work at being the best and try to motivate others so they achieve their potential. Remember my experience and continue to be open to new ones. Enjoy the nice things in life, but don't get my priorities screwed up. Believe in myself, be open and honest, and always continue to learn."*

In my fourth year of goal writing, I added that God was number one and His will and discernment were to be relied on. This was the year that I decided to follow God's will and started to develop a real relationship with Jesus. I learned that each year I wrote my goals, they crafted my purpose in life.

Writing down your goals is one of the most valuable actions you can take to craft a successful life. Goals help you maintain discipline and provide a clear vision. They transform a dream into reality and keep you motivated.

When you encounter roadblocks, your goals will inspire you to keep pushing forward and not give up. Here is a great list to help you create your life plan:

1. Write down your goals for the year.
2. Think deeply and then pray sincerely.
3. Create a vision and visualize it in your mind.

Discipline, self-control, and obedience are essential.

Dreaming big makes us feel vulnerable. It can be scary to dream big. What if the dream is a dumb idea? What if we fail? If we do, can we handle the disappointment? Many people are afraid to write down a goal because it feels too big.

I suggest seeking out a leader or someone you admire. Having a conversation with a real person, not just a therapist, can be very helpful. Talking to someone you respect could help you understand why you feel so afraid. When searching for someone to guide you, I find that the term "mentor" is often overused, so I hesitate to use it. I would prefer to think of this person as a colleague with whom I can have a conversation to help me overcome obstacles.

Consider a runner tackling hurdles: they will eventually reach their goal, but they must jump over each hurdle first. Engaging in a conversation could help you get past those hurdles. Most people are willing to help if you approach them honestly. If you ask someone for half an hour or an hour of their time to explain your goals and why you admire their achievements, they are likely to agree to help you.

It's essential to be genuine when asking for assistance; otherwise, you may not receive the support you need. Being authentic and honest requires humility, which can be difficult. But if you approach this correctly, seeking help doesn't have to be time-consuming. When I was transitioning to a full-time commission sales position, something I had no experience in, I went to three successful sales professionals and asked them what had helped them succeed. Their answers went into the blue folder, and I still have them today.

Planning is powerful, but only when we hold our plans with an open hand, recognizing that God is in control. He has redirected my written plans several times. My husband and I had been married for only a year, and we were living in Atlanta with no plans to move. A situation arose at work, and I was asked to move to Boulder, Colorado. We had to decide overnight. Once we said yes, I was gone three days later.

This experience influenced our life decisions for many years. God's hand was active and alive in this decision. When we said we would move, we did not know all the ins and outs of what this change in goals would look like, but we knew this risk was the right answer. Even with all the unknowns, we knew we were taking a good risk. When God is your partner in setting and modifying goals, it removes pressure from the situation. This surrender to God is not passive but an active decision to involve and trust Him.

Writing down my goals not only helps me connect with God but also enhances my creativity. If you take the time to write down your goals, it requires effort, thought, introspection, and an understanding of yourself and what you truly want. In this process, you tend to be more honest, as, since it's private, you're not performing for an audience. Writing your goals helps you learn a lot about yourself as you reflect on them.

I write out my schedule every night for the following day. Even though I have a digital calendar, writing it down helps me think more clearly. This is a quick process, but this simple planning exercise creates a clear road map for the next day. You know what you want to get done, and it helps you avoid forgetting an important phone call or meeting. You know how to pace your day so that, by the end, you've accomplished what you set out to do.

This process helps me discern God's will as I plan my day. However, I don't see these goals as set in stone; they can evolve as I gather new insights and decide to change direction based on what comes my way.

Reading scripture helps me receive guidance on what steps to take. One very helpful scripture I go to when making a decision or setting a goal is Ephesians 5:15–16: *"Look carefully then how you walk, not as unwise but as wise, making the best use of the time because the days are evil."*

I reflect on past experiences, take inventory of where I am now, and look forward to future hopes and dreams. This scripture helps eliminate confusion and gives me clarity on how to move forward. The process of looking back, examining the current situation, and then thinking about the future allows me to craft ideas and plans. It helps me discern if God is directing me to do something different.

By outlining even my daily plans, I set myself up to be more creative. With a plan in place, I can relax and focus on thinking deeply. This openness allows me to explore more colorful and innovative ideas rather than just move linearly from point A to point B.

I believe that when everything is written down, my mind is free to generate creative ideas. That's when I feel I can hear God's voice and the inspiration of the Holy Spirit guiding me. There's even research suggesting that writing with a pen or pencil engages your brain differently than typing does. Ultimately, I think these thoughts and insights I gain lead me closer to fulfilling the Lord's purpose in my life.

It's your life, and only you can live it. Consider all the time you spend on activities like buying concert tickets, grocery shopping, or other daily routines you often deem important. When you plan a trip, you take the time to map it out, but it's essential to remember that this is your life. Who are you going to spend the rest of your life with? How is it going to look? It's your life, and while you can create a vision for it, God's the one who will ultimately perfect it.

Let me repeat that. We don't need to achieve perfection. God will perfect our lives for us. However, we do have a responsibility. By putting effort into our work and carefully considering it, we are taking on some of that responsibility.

By creating plans, you'll learn a lot about yourself, and you'll be open to His guidance in significant ways. However, it requires effort and energy. It's not going to be a simple or effortless process where answers just appear. It takes work, and perhaps that's why many people avoid it.

For my first attempt at writing my goals and crafting a plan, I used a workbook and listened to tapes. Today, I use a goal workbook. I set goals annually and update my long-term plan.

I want to emphasize that, as you craft your life, it's crucial to be grounded in prayer and scripture. Without this foundation, the life you create may be more worldly and driven by the flesh, which

likely won't align with what God desires for you. When that happens, you'll probably feel disappointed and confused, not realizing that your life needs to be in tune with God's intentions. For believers, this concept will resonate more deeply. Unbelievers, however, may struggle to grasp it.

I started out looking for a career. I was just looking for a job that would pay enough for me to support myself. My motivations were very worldly; I was primarily focused on making money. It wasn't a refined approach because, at that point, my priorities were all about financial gain. However, being in a career-driven job was difficult for me. I was not happy. The work was not easy, and the time passed slowly.

I knew that my feelings, while not fully theological, were heartfelt and an attempt to align with God's will. Though I didn't completely understand it, I had a genuine desire to do so. My heart was one hundred percent.

Think about someone who chooses to live their life without any connection to God. If they decide to ignore God's will and create their own plan, ultimately that plan will not lead to true peace or joy. These are the two things that people genuinely seek, yet they can't just go to a store and buy them.

PRACTICE SESSION

Create some time on your calendar to build a three-year Kingdom Purpose Plan. This might be something that you have never done, but don't be nervous. Approach this process with a positive and prayerful attitude. This will help you be more creative.

Step 1: Pray for clarity.
Invite God to reveal what He wants your life to reflect three years from now.

Step 2: Identify your Kingdom priorities.
Some examples: relationships, generosity, calling, service, or spiritual growth.

Step 3: Write the vision.
One page, future-focused, written as if it is already happening.

Step 4: Translate it into annual and monthly goals.
Based on your list of kingdom priorities and your page on vision, document three to five annual goals and then break these down into monthly goals.

Step 5: Hold it with an open hand.

Reflection Prayer: *Our Father who art in heaven, please align my life to Your will. Give me the discipline to create a plan and the courage to work the plan. In the precious name of Jesus, Amen.*

CHAPTER 8

Money, Money, Money, but You Still Need to Steward It

"No one can serve two masters. For you will hate one and love the other; you will be devoted to one and despise the other. You cannot serve God and be enslaved to money."
– Matthew 6:24

When I worked at National Data Corporation, they invested in promising leadership candidates by sending them to a financial planning group as a perk. I was fortunate to be picked as one of these candidates.

I met with two men from the group, who reviewed my tax returns and other financial documents. They had an office in a professional office complex. The office was not flashy, but it was accommodating. I sat in a chair with the two men facing me. While examining my tax return, they noticed a significant amount in charitable contributions. They stopped and asked me, "Do you tithe?"

The first emotion that I felt when they asked this was embarrassment. You might think the normal emotion would be pride. They seemed so shocked that I felt I did not have their acceptance, or maybe I had done something wrong. I replied, "Yes, I do." The men were quite surprised, noting that this was uncommon among young people. At this point, they shared that they were both Christians and ran their business based on Christian principles.

I'm sharing this story not to seek praise but to illustrate that while money can be the root of all evil, it can also be used as a resource in God's Kingdom. You do not want to make money an idol; instead, you should use money for good. Being intentional about how you manage your finances is crucial.

This chapter isn't about wealth or poverty. It's about trust. Money tests who we serve: ourselves or God.

I understand the journey of going from having no money to being able to save and invest. Through years of chasing quotas, I realized a subtle shift was happening: money wasn't just a paycheck anymore; it was a mirror revealing my heart. The key that kept me grounded was recognizing that these financial opportunities were gifts from God; the money ultimately belonged to Him, not me. God expanded my platform and blessed me abundantly.

All of my work was commission-based, and to excel in that environment, I needed to prioritize money correctly. The focus should be on the client's needs and solving their problems, not just on earning a commission. People can easily tell if you are motivated solely by money. By adding value and genuinely solving problems, you will advance in your career.

When you're in a commission-based role focused on making money, money can become a yardstick for success. Success is often measured by how much money you make because of your commissions. It requires a careful balancing act to avoid getting too caught up in it. There were times when I did get caught up in the numbers.

When I worked at a corporation, I felt the pressure of the new sales goal each new year. I would be nervous, afraid I would fail. When I started my own company, I had no revenue or customers. I lived with a nervous pit in my stomach. As I grew, I felt responsible for the employees and wanted to keep growing. These emotions led me to work more than was healthy at times.

I can remember an event at the company I owned. It had grown to the point where I had revenue and customers. I was making a little money, but forty percent of my revenue came from one big client. This client was bought by a larger company, and they told me I was at risk of losing the business.

For weeks, I was seriously stressed. I could not calm down and did not know what to do. Luckily, I stopped long enough to hear the Holy Spirit. In my bathroom, while getting ready, I stopped and prayed to God, telling Him that whatever happened, the outcome was in His hands. I turned it over to Him. I felt less stress and more at peace.

The following day, I received a call from the corporate office of my one big client, who needed a quick response to a problem. My company reacted and asked me to meet with them, not only to keep the business I had but also to grow it. Situations like these, and there were more, showed me the value of service and having a peaceful mind.

For me, it's essential to remember that money is not just about personal gain or the things I can buy. I strive to view it as an investment in the future and maintain a long-term perspective. I often ask myself, *How can I use my money to help someone or support an organization in furthering God's Kingdom?*

God has provided me with opportunities that have translated into financial gain, which was ultimately my goal. It's clear to me that He has given me more than I ever thought necessary, and I see this as an issue of ownership. There are two types of ownership:

a. Ownership: The Illusion of Control
    a. This is the human tendency to believe we own what we earn, that we did it all, and that it was all within our power.

b. Stewardship: The Freedom of Surrender
    a. This is believing that everything is God's property. This view lifts anxiety and redirects your efforts and purpose.

The true owner of my wealth is God, not me. So, as I look around my house, I remind myself that it ultimately belongs to Him.

The dream of owning a farm started back in my teens. We lived next to my grandfather's farm, and I wanted a horse, but my grandfather would not allow that. This dream was born of anger. I said, "I will show you. I will have my own farm someday."

Many years later, I did get my farm, and it represented independence for me. Instead of having horses on my farm, I had sheep. I came to realize that this farm was more God's doing than my independence. I acknowledged that the farm was God's as well. In this context, if everything is God's and I am not the true owner, then I am merely a steward of these resources. My responsibility is to take care of them and to consider how I can use them for His purposes, rather than just for my own benefit.

I believe it is essential to be mindful of how I use what God has entrusted to me and to use it in a way that honors Him. Children from our church visited the farm. We hosted a wedding and several receptions, as well as a fundraiser for a group raising money for wells in Tanzania. The idea for the fundraiser started when a student was selling handmade papier-mâché necklaces to raise money for wells.

We had a discussion, and I asked, "How can we use the farm to help?" We decided to have a drive-in movie at the barn. We made a big screen out of PVC pipe and big insulation boards. We had a concession stand in the other barn, and the 4H offices allowed us to use their equipment. We sold popcorn, hot dogs, and drinks. We promoted the event, and people who did not even come donated to the event. The night of the event, we were blessed with no rain. We took mobile payments and parked people's cars in the fields, and then they walked to the barn to watch the movie.

One of the best learning lessons involved a five-gallon plastic watering bottle. There was a water faucet at the bottom of the hill. We would have people fill up the water bottle and carry the full water bottle up the hill. It was heavy! This was to help people understand what the women in Tanzania do every day. They went to the well and carried the water home two miles every day. Even the strong, young football players had trouble carrying the full water bottles.

Realizing that the farm is God's allowed us to use it with and for other people. This expanded my mind, imagination, and knowledge. My sense of blessing exploded beyond what I thought was possible.

I truly love the idea that nothing belongs to me; it all belongs to Him. I think realizing this truth about my possessions and wealth is vital. If every asset had a title block, God's name would appear on mine. Think of the deed for your house. It would have God's name and your name.

If this affects all of our assets, then the room you're sitting in, the house, and the car you drive are all gifts from Him. This belief shapes your daily choices: how you save and manage your money, how you give your money, and how you spend your money on yourself. You must ensure that you use these assets in ways that glorify Him rather than diminish His glory.

I invite you to think about this concept of God owning your assets. This might be a very foreign idea to you, or it might be very familiar. From these thoughts, develop a stewardship giving plan.

When you share the responsibility of an asset with God, you become its steward and gain an enormous amount of peace.

PRACTICE SESSION

Before beginning these steps, take a moment to reflect on the truth that everything we have ultimately belongs to God and that we are called to steward it faithfully.

Step 1: Reflect on ownership.
List what you own. In front of each, write *"God's."*

Step 2: Review your spending and giving.
Does each expenditure reflect your values or your fears?

Step 3: Create a simple stewardship plan.
Decide on a percentage or a proactive act of regular giving, plus one intentional act of generosity each month.

Step 4: Pray for alignment.
Invite God to remind you daily that what's His will always be enough.

Reflection Prayer: *Our Father, who art in heaven, hallowed be Thy name. Give us this day our daily bread. In the precious name of Jesus, Amen.*

CHAPTER 9

Leading with Love vs. Leading with Power

"Don't just pretend to love others, really love them.
Hate what is wrong; hold tightly to what is good."
– Romans 12:9

One of the most significant lessons I've learned came from one of my bosses at Global Payments. During my first employee review meeting, he asked me a shocking question: "What are your goals, and how can I help you achieve them?"

My boss was a New Yorker from Manhattan, a real, genuine New Yorker. You would never have thought that such a question would come out of his mouth. I was stunned by this question. It wasn't what I'd expected, and I could sense his seriousness and genuine desire to help me.

This approach was uncommon in corporate America during employee reviews; he truly led with love rather than power. Power and authority are most effective when used with genuine love, not raw power, to foster authentic growth. There is effective power in leading with genuine care. Do not erase the responsibility of power and authority that you own. Love combined with power and authority creates miracles.

Having two dogs can be a great way to train a puppy. The puppy learns by watching the older dog and mimicking its behavior. This same learning process can be applied to humans. Just like a puppy learning by watching an older dog, I was learning how love leads more powerfully than authority ever could. Observing someone who excels at something can provide you with valuable insights that you can apply to your growth. Learn from a good human.

When I moved into management and began conducting employee reviews, I made it a point to start with that very question. Asking this question allows you to learn a lot about a person and puts you in a better position to assist them and benefit your company. You'll gain insights into whether you have the right person in the right job. When someone feels that you genuinely care about their success, it builds a bond of trust. With that foundation of trust, you can ensure that the right people are in the right roles, leading to highly motivated employees and increased productivity.

However, in using Christlike leadership, there is a cost. A great example of this involves a work associate named Dave. This all happened years ago, when there weren't as many women in leadership positions. I became Dave's boss, which was challenging because I was younger than him and a woman. His reaction was one of horror; he was visibly upset that I was in charge. Dave and I had been friends, but once he heard this news, I could tell that he was not happy. Our communication came to almost a complete halt, and when we did communicate, it was hostile. He even said out loud, "I can't believe this has happened."

I wanted to yell, "I earned this, and this will be good for both of us in the end! Stop acting like a child!" but I did not. Despite his reaction, I approached the situation with empathy. I tried to understand his perspective instead of getting defensive.

I protected him in ways he was unaware of. There was a situation in which my boss wanted to transfer him to a position that would have negatively affected his family. I stood up for him, telling my boss that this couldn't happen. I went out on a limb for him because I knew that if he made this big move, he would not be given the reward he deserved. I knew that and could not do that to a person with a family. There were other options our company could implement to solve the problem.

It is a difficult thing when you have to go against your boss, and my boss was the CEO of the company. It hurt emotionally because of the analysis I had to do to figure it out. I had to make sure I could do this another way, without moving Dave and ending up with the same outcome. I also had to muster the courage to talk to my boss. It hurt politically because you never make points with the boss when you say "no."

After several years, when Dave eventually left the company, he told me that I was the best boss he had ever had. This is a clear example of how leading with love can yield long-term benefits. While the short term was certainly not easy, in the end, love prevailed. If I had reacted in a more typical manner, I might not have given him the opportunity to succeed. The opposite side of the coin was that my boss would work people until they dropped.

The story with Dave shows that leading with love can cost you in the short term but pay off in the long term. I had to be authentic to myself and to my company. I had to be real. Being authentic in your leadership style can have tangible benefits. If you develop your leadership style with authenticity, it creates a bond of trust, and people let their guard down a bit.

Fred Gumbel was in charge of a very large bank, and my company had tried to establish a relationship with him for years. The interesting part is that I didn't know they had been pursuing him for so long. I was quite naïve at the time, but I was eager and hungry.

One day, I decided to call him, and to my surprise, Fred Gumbel, a senior executive, answered the phone. I introduced myself and invited him to visit our network. He said he would be traveling through Atlanta and could stop by on a specific date. I rushed to inform my boss that Fred would be coming in, and my boss was astonished. He asked how I had managed to get him to agree to a meeting since we had been trying for years. I simply replied, "I picked up the phone, called him, and asked."

I didn't see things in terms of male or female; I focused on treating everyone, regardless of gender, with respect, dignity, and authenticity. When I approached Fred Gumbel, I think he was used to being courted in more tactical ways. Other important people may have tried to persuade him by placing too much emphasis on power or by framing their motives in a way that didn't genuinely address his interests.

In my case, I was naïve and straightforward. I led with honesty rather than power. As a result, he agreed to meet, and that meeting eventually evolved into one of our largest exclusive relationships, worth a significant amount to the company over the years. I'm not entirely sure how others approached him before, but I believe my authentic approach made a difference.

If I had known that he was such an important guy, I might not have picked up the phone and called him. Sometimes, ignorance is bliss. There is real power in being led with genuine care. I think Fred knew I cared, and he learned that I cared for his company's interest.

Being a woman is a great asset, so don't trade in your femininity for something of lesser value. Women have a unique gift: an exceptional ability to have great instincts, form relational connections, and have strong work ethics. The difference in appearance between men and women plays a role in this dynamic. During my time in corporate America, I approached my appearance with modesty and professionalism while still embracing my femininity.

I don't view femininity as something to sacrifice; instead, I use it as a source of empowerment. There's great value in having men and women collaborate. You truly get the best of both worlds. I wouldn't want to work solely with women or solely with men. When both genders work together toward a common goal, the synergy can yield outstanding results. Genuine love will beat fake power. Don't be afraid to be yourself.

PRACTICE SESSION

Love is always a risk and takes energy to put into action, but you get so much more growth from it than when you use raw power. This concept is not the norm and might feel a bit foreign to you. So, I invite you to consider this path. Think of an experience and what the outcome would have been if you had handled the situation in a different way, a more loving way.

Here is an outline to define your leadership style using Christ's model:

Step 1: Reflect on your default mode.
When do you rely on authority or control instead of relationship?

Step 2: Identify a "Dave moment" in your life.
Where could you choose empathy over ego this week?

Step 3: Write your " Leadership Creed"
One or two sentences that describe how you want to lead like Christ.

Step 4: Pray for the "Fruit of the Spirit" in leadership
Specifically, patience, gentleness, and self-control.

Reflective prayer: *Our Father who art in heaven, thank You for the words, and the greatest of these is love. Empower me to put this into action. In the precious name of Jesus, Amen.*

This chapter ends **Part II: The Big Game: Staying True When the World Pulls Hard**. The world will seduce you with fear, money, ambition, rejection, and pressure. Storms, setbacks, and opportunities reveal what you truly believe. This is where practice and theory come together in real life. This is where the game is played. This is where you need God to be your coach.

I hope you are able to apply these ideas to your life events and learn. This process will reveal your strengths and shortcomings. Be willing to take the time to face the truth and your fears. Put in the time, practice, and discipline.

PART III

THE VICTORY WALK: LIVING LIKE YOU'VE ALREADY WON

One of my most fun and profitable jobs was with the start-up company Nova, now Elavon. I held several positions during this adventure, including senior VP of national sales. The end of the year is a big time in sales because you see the scoreboard and know if your team won or lost. One year, I knew that the team had performed well and we'd hit our numbers.

We won, and there was an awards party. I did not know what all the details were, but I knew enough to buy a beautiful new suit, and I walked into that meeting knowing I was the leader who had won. They invited my husband, so I knew it would be a bigger-than-normal celebration. It felt great! I did not feel pressure; I did not remember the difficult conflicts. The pit in my stomach was gone, and the stress was relieved. I walked onto that stage with a pep in my step, knowing I had won.

Section III marks a shift from learning who you are and how to trust God to living in the knowledge that you belong to Him. You are now walking in victory, not striving for it. Your faith is settled.

It is important for me to clarify what victory really means.

Victory is not:

- Money
- Applause
- Ease
- Control

Victory is:

- Faithfulness
- Obedience
- Endurance
- Stewardship
- Alignment with God
- Acceptance of Jesus as the Son of God

Victory is not the absence of struggle. It is the presence of peace in the middle of it.

Now, let's review where we have been and what comes next.

Part I was about identity: *Who you are*

Part II was about integrity: *How you live and what you believe*

Part III is about legacy: *What you leave behind and how you walk daily*

Part III views your life through the lens of eternal perspective. Living your life as if you've already won changes your definition of:

- Work
- Money
- Motherhood
- Leadership

- Success

You become less impressed by titles and more anchored in truth.

In my story about my sales award, my victory walk was just for that moment. The sales clock reset to zero. This third part of the book, "The Victory Walk," is about a posture, not just a moment.

Victory is not the outcome of one event; it is a way of walking:

- It's how you show up to work.
- It's how you handle relationships.
- It's how you value people.
- It's how you measure success.
- It's how you give.

Victory is daily, quiet, faithful, and obedient.

- Not flashy
- Not loud
- Not performed
- But powerful

Here's a preview of Part III – The Victory Walk:

Chapter 10: Win by Driving Your Red Truck Well

- Walking humbly in the work God has entrusted to you.
- Understanding that excellence is worship.
- Loving what you've been given rather than envying what others have.

Chapter 11: The Jobs That Really Matter

- Reclaiming motherhood, nurturing, mentoring, and the presence of holy work.
- Redefining influence through relationship, not power.

Chapter 12: Having Enough to Give It Away

- Learning to live with open hands.
- Seeing time, money, and energy as tools of generosity, not possessions.

Chapter 13: The Truth About Success

- Letting go of the world's scoreboard.
- Measuring life by alignment, not achievement.
- Discovering that joy does not come from accumulation but from purpose.

As you read Part III, it is important to anchor yourself to this truth: you don't have to prove anything, you don't have to outperform anyone, and you don't have to earn what was already given.

This victory is not earned; it is a gift to be received.

CHAPTER 10
Win by Driving Your Red Truck Well

"Work willingly at whatever you do, as though you were working for the Lord rather than for people."
– Colossians 3:23

I was very fortunate because my husband decided to move us from Atlanta to a small town. The town we chose was where I grew up, allowing me to experience adult life surrounded by my family.

When you return to the town where you were born, you often run into many people you know. One such encounter was with someone whose name I can't remember, but I recall our conversation vividly.

I was walking into the Kroger grocery store and had not made it past the cart station when I ran into an old high school acquaintance. It was exciting for me to be recognized by someone familiar to me; this did not happen in Atlanta. It made me feel welcome, surprised, and happy.

They greeted me and said, "Hello! I didn't know you were living back in Paducah." They went on to reminisce about my dad dropping me off at high school. Then they remarked, "I bet you were embarrassed getting out of that truck every day."

I couldn't believe what I was hearing because I had never felt embarrassed. I told them, "No, I felt loved." My dad never let the emotion of embarrassment into that truck. He shut embarrassment out with love. He did this by placing greater importance on function than position, valuing relationships over image. He showed me how much he valued me through the time invested during those drives to school. His love was expressed because he was not embarrassed.

That truck was an important work tool. It was strong and equipped, and it did not need to be shiny. He was proud and joyful. We laughed often in that truck. He also gave me instructions, showing me he cared about helping me. These rides to school in my dad's work truck crafted my view on worth and success. Every ride taught me that it is the true things that count, not the image.

My dad told me every day not to walk on the grass because that was what sidewalks were for, and he always reminded me that he loved me. That's all I remember. This experience illustrates the contrast between a worldly narrative and an eternal perspective.

In playing the game of life, you win when you have an eternal perspective. That's what my dad instilled in me while we rode in that truck. He had the attitude that he had already won and didn't need to impress anyone with material wealth, flashy cars, or social status. One truly wins the game of life only by adopting an eternal perspective that values everlasting spiritual rewards over fleeting worldly gains.

This red truck symbolized much more than just a means of getting me to school. Let me describe it in a bit more detail. Picture a truck from the 1950s. It was a dull red, not particularly striking, and lacked air conditioning. You rolled the windows down with a crank handle. What made it special were the two big black tires tied or chained to the front bumper, resembling two large eyeballs staring at you.

The plainness of the truck was its superpower. The function of the truck stomped out the idea that you needed flash to be effective. The purpose of the truck outweighed the fact that it was not beautiful. The superpower of this truck reflected quiet excellence, faithful obedience, and everyday victory.

My dad was a mechanic, and this truck was one of the tools he used to serve people, not to impress them. He would stop to help anyone he saw in need: stranded cars, overheated vehicles, and cars with flat tires. The tires on the front allowed him to push disabled cars without damaging them.

I spent a lot of time at the garage, and I can remember conversations my dad would have with customers. He would explain what the issue was and then provide options to resolve the problem. One option might be to buy a new car and replace it, and the other to repair what was already there. Option A could cost more than option B. He considered the customer's situation and tried to help financially by offering options. He was honest with them, and they kept coming back.

I can remember when my dad was in his eighties and had retired. He and I would go out to dinner, and we often saw his former customers. He would say, "I worked on that car," and he could remember the make and model. He would greet them, and it brought a smile to his face. My dad loved what he did. He was good at it and genuinely worked hard to take care of people. Many of the stops he made occurred after quitting hours, so it wasn't always about the clock; it was about service.

My hope is that someday, when you are in your eighties, you can look back with passion and pride, reflecting on your work with a smile and a sense of enjoyment. Remember to love what you do and do it well. Additionally, always keep in mind that relationships are important; adhere to the golden rule.

May you drive your red truck well and remember the real stuff, the eternal stuff, not the worldly stuff. My dad knew he had already won the battle.

It's important to recognize that everything we do should be approached with purpose and a sense of responsibility. If we view our work as being for the Lord, with Him as our boss and CEO, it comes with certain expectations, one of which is excellence.

Excellence doesn't have to be complex; it simply means doing our work well, completely, and thoughtfully. Whether you are running an errand for a neighbor by going to the grocery store or preparing a presentation as a young CEO for your company's annual kickoff event, striving for excellence is key.

When you adopt this attitude, it influences your entire mindset and approach to getting things done. Moreover, it encourages you to treat others with respect and kindness and to be truthful in all your interactions. These qualities are essential when working for the Lord, as they add depth and purpose to your tasks.

Even if no one is watching, whether you're performing a task solo or not on a public stage, remember that God sees your efforts. You are ultimately working for Him, which makes your work meaningful and inspires you to do it to the best of your ability.

And it doesn't matter if it's a little job or a big one. If you're a mother at home doing work no one sees, a COO, a leader of a team, a mechanic, or a CEO, it really doesn't matter. Focus on excellence, completeness, respect, kindness, and truth, no matter what you're doing.

Being authentic is closely related to the idea of working for or with the Lord. To be authentic means being true to yourself and your values, which requires a solid understanding of what those values are. Excellence is how you work, whereas authenticity is how you stand. Authenticity frees us from the comparison trap, giving us freedom from performance. Lastly, authenticity gives us real comfort in who we are, our identity.

Authenticity involves staying true to your beliefs rather than conforming to a culture or the beliefs of the world around you. This can be challenging. It's one thing to uphold your values in a private setting, but it's much tougher when you're in a large company or a public environment.

To cultivate authenticity, you need to practice it and make it a habit. It's essential to genuinely believe in your values so that embracing them becomes second nature. You shouldn't feel the need to pretend to be someone you're not or apologize for who you are. Instead, focus on being your authentic self without comparing yourself to others.

My dad didn't care; he simply drove his truck and focused on his plan. He knew he had won. He was genuine and authentic. It didn't bother him to think about whether he measured up to anyone else. His truck might not have been as nice, but that didn't make him feel inferior.

My value is in the Lord, and when push comes to shove, I can say "no" to other people. That isn't where my value comes from.

It's so important to recognize the value we receive from the Lord. When you truly understand your value and share it with others, you start to see everyone around you as a creation of God. Instead of comparing yourself to others or measuring your worth against theirs, you begin to respect and love them for who they are.

This perspective changes everything. It enhances your ability to listen, improves your leadership skills, and makes you a better boss. It enriches every interaction because you view everyone, no matter how challenging they may be, as a creation of God.

The dynamics change, as believing in someone alters the perspective needed to get things done. It's essential to recognize that no one is worthless or insignificant. After all, they are a creation made by God.

To distill this thought of identity: You are who you are because of God. No one gets to define it, and it can never be lost. Victory is settled.

PRACTICE SESSION

Use your imagination and picture yourself at age eighty. Where will you live, and what color will your hair be?

Step 1: Answer these questions:

- What do you hope people remember the most?
- What mattered the most?
- Did you love well?
- Did you show up faithfully?

Step 2: Take some time with your journal and journal on excellence:

- Authenticity
- Service
- Truth

Reflection Prayer: Our *Father, who art in heaven and created the bright stars and holds them in the dark sky, there are so many roads to drive and so many different roads to take. Please help me drive my red truck with authentic excellence to get to the destination of Your will. In the precious name of Jesus, Amen.*

CHAPTER 11
The Jobs That Really Matter

"Her children stand and bless her; her husband praises her."
– Proverbs 31:28

I had a wonderful mother. She was the best! Because of her example, I developed a positive view of motherhood. She was a businesswoman but also a devoted mother. I always assumed I would become a mother one day, and I viewed that role as a significant responsibility.

My view was truly more than an assumption; I expected to be a mother. My reality was that I would be a mother. There was no plan B or plan C. I had watched all the women in my family become mothers, and I did not see life without motherhood and a family. There was never a consideration of not having a family. I was 110 percent confident that I would have a family.

Mike and I got married in our mid-thirties, and I had no concerns about starting a family. I never considered that there might be challenges. However, I was hit hard when I lost my first baby, followed by losing three more. We were living in Atlanta when I had my first pregnancy, and I had the best doctor, Dr. Taylor. I was about twelve weeks along, and we called Dr. Taylor because I had some spotting. I called my mom and Aunt Julie, and they told me not to worry, as this can happen.

The doctor had me come in for an ultrasound. I knew something was up when he called us back to his office. He told us we had lost the baby. This moment was when my expectation became a different reality. The pain, the hurt, the unbelief that this could happen. It was not a good day.

As women, we possess the incredible ability to create life. Imagine what our world would look like if every woman embraced motherhood as a miracle and a gift. Yet, our culture has convinced women that a corporate job is more valuable than being a mother, urging us to trade a job for a miracle.

What would our society be like if it truly valued motherhood and supported that belief responsibly? The impact of motherhood has far-reaching, eternal implications. Our societies would not be so self-focused. There would be more and stronger families. Future generations would be shaped by love and virtue rather than relentless productivity. You would find legacy, not productivity. Motherhood is not just a role; it is an eternal work that creates a legacy. I firmly believe that motherhood is the most influential role there is.

Blending motherhood and career means that there will be tension. It is a lot to handle. The value of motherhood does not diminish meaningful work. It just means you could need help, you might become a better planner, and you might get in the habit of being an early riser. Worth comes from God, not a role, and no title outranks raising a soul.

While Mike and I did not have our own children, God blessed us in many other ways. We redirected our loss into other areas, and we found many blessings and healing. We are so grateful that we didn't get stuck in our grief but looked to God for more. Motherhood is not only biological; it is relational, spiritual, and eternal. We taught Sunday school to high school students for eleven years, attended church camp with the kids, and used our farm for various activities. Currently, we're teaching fourth-grade boys at our church.

Several years ago, our church hired a young woman to lead the girls' youth group. The church asked if she could live with us while she looked for an apartment, estimating it would be about two weeks. We were complete strangers to one another. However, we both agreed to it.

Eventually, those two weeks turned into two years, and what a blessing Anna was in our lives!

Our first two weeks were spent getting to know each other. We got her all moved in and settled. We would all go to work and have dinner together. We would talk, laugh, and learn about each other. The two weeks were very different but comfortable.

When the two weeks were up, we said, "Let's try two months." After two months, we all said, "Let's keep going." It was at that point that the temporary turned into a family. That Christmas, Anna gave us a painting that said, *"Home is where your heart is."* It was very special to us, and it signaled to me that God had truly blessed our lives with Anna.

During her time with us, she met and dated her current husband, whom Mike taught with in Sunday school. Anna and Matt went on to have three children, and we became very involved in their lives, participating in activities like Upward Basketball, soccer, and T-ball. Every Christmas, we would make a birthday cake for Jesus.

Anna and her family enriched our lives in so many wonderful ways. We were able to share life with Anna and also got to know her whole family. When they came to visit, they stayed at our house. What great times we had with her family, and they filled our home with love, laughter, and prayer. Anna became a great mother. She fully understands the miracle and gift of motherhood. Sometimes, our prayers are answered in surprising ways.

These experiences show that Mike and I didn't receive exactly what we prayed for, but we got more. Due to nature, we were simply too old to have our own children, but God blessed us with many other children in our lives. The blessings came in God's timing, not ours, so there were many dry patches of grief.

It is important to honor grief without rushing the healing. It takes time and prayer. During these patches of grief, I experienced anger, confusion, and disappointment. I can remember just feeling so blue and sad. I just could not shake it off. It lingered. I still had to go to work and live life, but sadness followed me around like a shadow. I had to wrestle with this grief.

Just because you have faith, it does not mean you will not have sorrow. Faith does not eliminate sorrow. You can easily become consumed by your pain and fail to recognize the blessings it brings. After experiencing the loss of children and going through infertility treatments, Mike and I encountered numerous challenges. It's easy to get caught up in that pain and hold on to it, but at some point, you need to release it, let it go, and trust that the Lord will bless you, and He will.

The blessings may not come in the form you initially expected, but they are still significant. We have had the opportunity to interact with so many children in ways we might not have if we had started our own family.

I know that struggling to have children can be incredibly painful and isolating for many people. It's a topic that often goes unspoken, and many people might not even realize it is affecting others. You certainly wouldn't bring it up during dinner conversations because no one wants to hear about it, and you would often end up feeling stares of discomfort from others.

It feels like there's a silent grief out there for those going through this experience. I want to share that there is hope and blessings and that life can still be good. It may not look exactly the way you envisioned, but it can still be fulfilling in its own special way.

"All these people earned a good reputation because of their faith, yet none of them received all that God had promised. For God had something better in mind for us, so that they would not reach perfection without us" (Hebrews 11:39–40). This scripture sets our eyes on the eternal, not the present. This message helps us avoid getting stuck in our grief. We can trust that God has something better, and this is a promise that will come true if you put your faith in Him. Do not resign yourself to your circumstance, but cling to this statement of redemption.

PRACTICE SESSION

The action item for this chapter is to write a legacy letter. A legacy letter is a document you write to family, friends, or future generations to share your story, values, and wisdom. Reflect on what you want to leave behind, such as life lessons, family traditions, and core beliefs.

Step 1: Consider writing your legacy letter:

- To the children you've had
- To the children you never had
- To the future

Step 2: Remember to include:

- What you wish someone had told you
- What matters most to you
- What must never be forgotten
- What was worth the cost to you
- What God taught you through pain

Reflection Prayer: *Our Father, who art in heaven, who holds the bright stars in the dark sky. I am grateful that You are my rock and my Father who listens to my cries. You do not condemn or become impatient. You listen with a heart that is full of bold love. You answer my cries in ways that are heavenly, not earthly. Let me keep my eyes fixed on the eternal, not on the present. Thank You, Father. In the precious name of Jesus, Amen*

CHAPTER 12

Having Enough to Give It Away

"And God will generously provide all you need. Then you will always have everything you need and plenty left over to share with others."
– 2 Corinthians 9:8

I loved work, so I did a lot of it, and I did it well. My career developed, and I sold the second company I founded. There are many documents executed when you sell a company. Many companies want owners to stay on for a certain period of time to learn from their experience. I had an employee contract in my package. I knew that my employment contract contained serious non-compete clauses and a term for my employment. The contract was in writing, but I expected something else.

I did not love being an employee again, but I did love the game of business and being part of the team. I expected they would keep me beyond my contract. They did not, and the termination of the contract became a reality. This termination was my responsibility. I negotiated the terms but was still surprised.

One day, I was an employee with a jam-packed calendar; the next, I was not an employee, and I had a very open calendar. The silence of the first morning with a new rhythm was empty and hollow. I had to find a new rhythm.

I came to see retirement as a matter of changing gears. The things, events, and time in life simply become different. When you're in full-time work mode, there isn't much flexible time available to create different events in your life.

This transition is often what scares people who are considering retirement or a change in their work life. With a full-time job, your calendar is automatically filled with necessary tasks to fulfill your responsibilities. You have a routine. However, once you change gears, your calendar opens up, and you have the opportunity to create your own day.

For those of you balancing full-time work and raising kids, you might be eagerly waiting for this moment. If you're thinking about this transition, take some time to consider how you want to spend your time. If you've already changed gears, reflect on how you are using your time and consider making adjustments.

This can be a challenging task, and the transition from work to an empty calendar can be stressful. Often, you are moving from an important role to having no importance or authority. Expect things to feel very different and that you will have to struggle through them, but don't cave to the stress.

Change your gears and manage the process. As a way to categorize, here are the **Three Gears of Kingdom Living:**

- **Provision Gear:** Working to meet needs. Paying the bills, saving for the future, and taking care of emergencies.
- **Purpose Gear**: Working to serve God and others.
- **Peace Gear:** Using time generously for eternal things.

As your calendar frees up and there might not be as much of the Provision Gear, pray and consider what the new rhythm could be. To fill that time, dedicate yourself to serving others, invest in the lives of other people, disciple others to know Jesus and study the Bible, volunteer your time, or start and nurture a hobby you love.

I still work, but not full-time. This part-time work has given my calendar freedom. I serve on several boards that I believe in, both the people involved and the organizations' missions. I also volunteer at a local organization that provides food and clothing to those in need. Each week, I dedicate a couple of hours to filling food boxes. My husband and I teach a fourth-grade boys' Sunday school class at church. I lead an online D Group created by Tara-Leigh Cobble. I have also committed to playing golf, which is a challenge but is possible with more time available. Other hobbies I enjoy include gardening, reading, and knitting.

I don't share these activities with you so you can replicate them; instead, I want to illustrate how the gears of life can shift. I am spending more time in the Purpose Gear and Peace Gear. Your gifts, passions, and activities will look different, but I can assure you that investing your time in unpaid service will make you feel incredibly rich. You will be blessed by helping and investing in others.

One of my first experiences of giving something without expecting anything in return was in middle school. I have an aunt, Julie, who is only four years older than me, and we grew up like sisters. Our mothers worked together. Once, when my aunt got sick, I heard about it. I had a birthday party to attend at a roller rink, but I chose not to go so that I could help Julie, since her mom was at work and couldn't be there. I skipped the party, stayed with her, and didn't tell anyone. I did have a moment of hesitation about helping her because missing the fun was something I really did not want to experience. In the end, though, I picked service over fun.

The result of this decision was that, for the first time, I realized that giving changes you more than the person you helped. This formed the seed of my belief that generosity feels like abundance, not loss. Looking back, I am glad I did not pick fun over service. I would have missed a big life lesson.

Later, my aunt found out that I had missed the party to take care of her, and she was so thankful. She couldn't believe I had done that for her. It might sound small, but for a kid, those birthday parties felt really important.

I remember how it made me feel: full and fulfilled. I knew I was doing the right thing, and it felt good. That was probably one of the very first times I did something for someone without expecting anything in return.

It is best not to just give money away; you need to use wisdom when you do. It is important for people to understand money and its mechanisms. Everyone needs to manage their finances well and take care of their money.

It's similar to the instructions given on an airplane: if you need oxygen, you should put on your own mask first before helping someone else. You can't give away your oxygen and then expect to help others effectively.

I am thankful that we did not spend our savings. Because we saved, Mike and I were able to buy four hundred Gideon Bibles and give them away at a Halloween event. We placed a Life Savers candy on each and handed them all out in thirty minutes. The kids were so excited. I can remember one little boy saying, "Look, Mom, my very own Bible."

The same principle applies to money. You need to ensure that you are financially stable and secure before giving away your resources. In this life, we have bills to pay, the church to donate to, and basic needs to meet.

It's crucial to be responsible with your finances and manage your money wisely. If you do, you will be able to help others without putting yourself or your family at risk.

Recognizing this truth is important. You do not want to run out of oxygen. There are other ways to give than just money. You can give your time, energy, and experience. This can have a more profound effect on your heart than just giving money. You learn compassion and what it feels like to be in someone's shoes.

Giving your time can be a valuable way to contribute without jeopardizing your financial stability. You don't have to give everything away; instead, you should strive for a balance and understand how to manage your resources effectively. The Holy Spirit will work in your heart to cultivate contentment and the realization that real joy comes from eternal investments, not earthly ones.

The Lord calls us to be responsible and to help others. When you are prudent and grow your financial resources, you'll be in a better position to help more people. Conversely, if you squander your money and fail to manage it well, you'll struggle to assist anyone, much like how you wouldn't be able to assist others if you ran out of oxygen.

This requires wisdom and a basic understanding of personal finance. You don't need to take a formal finance class, but there are some fundamental principles and techniques that are essential to know. There are classes, books, and websites you can find through Google or AI. I also refer people to Dave Ramsey. He does a great job teaching personal finance. For a basic household, this might include:

1. Calculate your monthly income.
    a. Figure out your take-home pay after taxes and deductions.

   b. If your income fluctuates, average it over the last three to six months for an estimate.

2. Track your spending manually using a notebook or utilize software or an app. I use Intuit products, but there are many.
   a. Categorize into (1) Needs (essentials), (2) Wants (discretionary), such as dining out, entertainment, hobbies, and shopping, (3) Debt, (4) Savings, and (5) Charity/Church
   b. Categorize your main household expense categories, e.g., rent/mortgage, utilities, insurance…

3. Create a budget.
   a. Simple Budgeting Rule: 50 percent goes to needs, 30 percent goes to wants, and 20 percent goes to savings and extra debit payments. Be sure to add your tithe to your church. There are many plans; this is one example.

4. Build positive habits.
   a. Automate what you can by setting up auto payments for bills and savings. Pay yourself first.
   b. Review monthly.
   c. Cut out non-essentials such as unused subscriptions.

Reading the Bible and reflecting on its stories encourages us to embrace kindness and caring for others. The feelings we get from these acts of generosity are truly priceless.

You're blessed to be a blessing. True abundance is not defined by endless accumulation but by reaching a state of "having enough" that naturally enables generous giving.

PRACTICE SESSION

Create a Kingdom Stewardship Plan using the following practical, faith-based framework for managing your resources or your time, talent (abilities/gifts), and treasures (finances and material assets):

Step 1: Annual budget.
Create a clear picture of how the resources God has entrusted to you are being used. Identify what goes toward needs, savings, giving, and margin so you can care for your responsibilities while still being able to bless others. Wise stewardship in the Provision Gear makes generosity possible. Apply a prayerful attitude and planning.

Step 2: Service audit
Review and write down how your time is currently spent during a typical week. Notice how much time is devoted to Provision, Purpose, and Peace, and consider where adjustments could create more opportunities to serve others and invest in eternal things.

Step 3: Generosity calendar.
Choose one or two consistent ways to serve others and place them on your calendar. Planning these opportunities helps generosity become a regular rhythm of life rather than just a good intention.

Many churches offer classes, budget tools, and study groups on kingdom stewardship. Creating and implementing these plans allows for freedom from debt, deeper trust in God, and joy of participating in His work.

Reflection Prayer: *Our Father, who art in heaven, where do You want me to give? Where do You want me to serve? Please direct me with wisdom and discernment. In the precious name of Jesus, Amen.*

CHAPTER 13
The Truth About Success

"But among you, it will be different. Whoever wants to be a leader among you must be a servant."
– Matthew 20:26

One piece of information about me that you might not guess is that I was once a sheep farmer. When I built the barn for my sheep, I transformed the loft area into a business office. When you enter a typical office, you usually walk through a foyer with plants and glass before getting to the stairs or elevator.

At my office, you opened a door that led to a barn with stalls for sheep and barn cats sleeping away. You walked to the door on the opposite wall and walked upstairs. When you arrived on the upper level and opened the door, it looked like a typical office: desks, lateral files, computers, a water cooler, and windows. The UPS man could see baby lambs being born downstairs and a busy business office upstairs.

One of the key benefits of my business was that we did our own customer service. We did not outsource this, and AI had not yet been created. This office can be reached quickly from my home in the event of a serious issue. I could react faster. Initially, I did not talk about the office publicly and wanted to be more secretive about it. I was afraid the office would create an unprofessional image for my business, but over time, this idea evaporated.

One of my large partners was the leading bank in town, and they wanted to feature me in their magazine. They sent a photographer, and I dressed in my best black business suit and pearls. I figured he would take the picture upstairs in my office. He did not. He wanted the picture in the barn. I was sitting on bales of straw with a barn cat beside me. He asked me, "Can you hold one of the baby lambs?" I did, and he took the picture.

The office was no longer a secret; it was published. Customers loved it, people loved it, and freedom was born from this. The farm was a special place, and God used it in special ways. Because I had great employees, a good business plan, and experience, we created a great business and were given the freedom to be different. These employees were also changed by our life in a barn. They gave me a beautiful photograph with the scripture from Ephesians 3:20 added: *"Now all glory to God, who is able, through His mighty power at work within us, to accomplish infinitely more than we might ask or think."* This was a gift that I greatly treasured.

This decision was atypical and involved some risk. This unconventional office setup telegraphed a different way to do things. Remember, there are multiple definitions of success. Be on alert that my words on success could challenge the cultural scorecard version.

It was essential for me that my goals and business plan aligned with the values of Jesus. Riding a tandem bike with Jesus is countercultural to the world. When you infuse your business plan with Jesus' values, it becomes powerful and authentic. This is the truth about success. The business did grow, and I eventually moved to a larger, more traditional location, but the office in the barn's loft was creative and enjoyable; it was a significant point on my journey.

How we define success greatly influences how we approach our work. I group success in three categories:

- Worldly
- Business
- Eternal

The intent of this chapter is to help you reevaluate which scoreboard you are using. Jesus defines success in very different terms than our culture: *"For even the Son of Man came not to be served but to serve others and to give his life as a ransom for many"* (Mark 10:45). Putting an office in a sheep barn might not seem successful to some people, but it worked for me. Success is how you define it.

Are you aiming for worldly success, business success, or eternal success? The contrast is clear: worldly success is marked by ego, money, and personal advancement. Business success is defined by numbers, data, and money. Eternal success focuses on humility, resourcefulness, Kingdom purpose, and servitude.

Understanding these differences is crucial. Reflect on your actions and their implications. Moreover, it's important to understand the business skills, techniques, and methods necessary to foster a successful business. You cannot simply fake your way to business success.

Building a business was a real process, and I have spent a significant amount of my life working hard, often to the point of imbalance. At times, I worked too much; I was consumed by work. I view these times as seasons.

There are intentional seasons where work might consume a high percentage of your time, but this does not last; it is a season. It is important to maintain a balance in life, but be aware that there may be intentional seasons when there is more work than play. Hard work is not a problem, but working without awareness or purpose is. You need to know why you are pushing so hard. The "why" is vitally important.

My shepherding provides great examples of different work seasons. Sheep eat grass, so you don't even need to feed them. So, for the majority of the time, the work is even and not very intense. The big event for the sheep is that you have to have them sheared every year. This is a very intense day.

I have realized that I have some weaknesses in the area of balance, but I would not have changed anything. I feel I understand why. When I was in Atlanta, I was part of a group that founded a company and took it public on the New York Stock Exchange. It was a significant amount of work, and I was dedicated to my job. Two of my girlfriends even staged an intervention, expressing their concern that I was working too much and would eventually harm myself.

At the time, I told them that this phase wouldn't last forever and that I had a plan. I instinctively knew it was temporary. I believe that if you have a plan, are aware of it, and are open to guidance, that is one of the key factors in success. However, if you don't have a plan and are merely working for the sake of working, you can become trapped in that cycle, like a hamster on a wheel, going nowhere continuously.

Analyze if you are working with a plan or reactively. Is your work a purposeful effort or endless motion? Do you believe your work is driven by fear or obedience? Working a plan, having a purpose, and being obedience-driven are all items that fuel success in a positive way and eliminate burnout.

Having a plan helps you understand why you're working and what your goals are. Knowing what steps you need to take (X, Y, and Z) to achieve your objectives and where that will lead you can provide a sense of structure. This approach helps create a more intentional way of working.

Marrying my husband gave my life greater purpose. I desired to spend time with Mike and at home. My marriage changed the way I allocated my time. I did not want to travel as much or spend weekends at the office. I still had to do this, but my desire changed. Creating this gauge made me notice my previous, full-court press of working all the time. My idea of success began to include relationships, family, presence, and a shared life.

This was an evolution and involved timing. It was just a different time, but it did not make the past seasons wrong. I did not regret my past working habits, but I did feel gratitude for my new marriage and relationship. Mike helped me slow down a bit. Just having him in my life made me want that change. It was part of an evolution and a process that I didn't want to stop.

For those who are currently navigating this process or trying to create something, you need to have awareness and a plan. You don't want to simply give all your time to work without understanding the reason behind it.

Founding the company was intense, but we had a plan and a great team, and by God's grace, we achieved our goal. Our team took the company public, and we got to be on the floor of the New York Stock Exchange to watch it happen. Not many people get that opportunity, but we did.

I remember saying after that experience, "I'll never start another company again," because I had worked so hard. However, I ended up starting something else anyway. Part of that drive comes from my love for creating things. We all have different gifts, and I believe God has given us a variety of talents. I happen to have a lot of energy, which is essential for being an entrepreneur. But it really depends on what gifts you possess.

Worldly advancement and Kingdom purpose are two distinct focuses. Worldly advancement can be measured in terms of status, money, and title, essentially the scoreboard for success in business. These aspects (status, money, and influence) are all tied to worldly ideals.

Kingdom purpose can be measured in spiritual fruit and character growth. Track increases in love, joy, peace, patience, kindness, goodness, faithfulness, gentleness, and self-control. Monitor your character to see if you realize more contentment, peace, and joy. Kingdom success often looks smaller, slower, and less impressive at first. The Kingdom-purpose idea of success runs counter to societal expectations and worldly advancement.

It's essential to be in sync with Jesus and align your life with His guidance, even though that may go against cultural norms. Without this alignment, you might reach the end of your journey and look back wishing you had done things differently, that you hadn't prioritized your job so much, especially if it meant sacrificing time with your family. So, I believe that being in harmony with Jesus and understanding your role is vital to your overall plan.

On the other hand, Kingdom-purpose ideals involve the unique gifts that God has given each of us. Each person has their own set of gifts. While some gifts may be similar, everyone generally has a unique combination.

When you prayerfully seek to use these gifts, you will find rewards in the Kingdom, which I refer to as Kingdom purposes. These pursuits lead to more eternal successes, reflecting a broader, more lasting perspective than mere immediate achievements highlighted on billboards.

Achieving these eternal goals requires understanding your gifts and committing to using them wisely. This process takes time: time to pray and time to ask God for guidance, wisdom, and direction. It's important to have an awareness of your gifts, even if you don't fully understand them at first.

Take some time to think about what energizes you. What gets you excited, the thing that moves you without manufactured motivation? What are the things that you feel called to create or steward? These are areas where you will feel you have real purpose. Where are you chasing someone else's version of success and not being true to yourself?

It takes time to understand your gifts; no one can do it for you. You need to take the time to build a relationship with God and pray to Him. He will answer your prayers, I promise you. He will answer anyone's prayers.

I think the biggest myth about success is that money will make you happy. People often believe that money can buy things that bring them joy, but that's simply not true. We've seen countless examples of Hollywood celebrities, athletes, and others who have had an abundance of wealth, much more than most of us can imagine, yet they still struggle with happiness.

True happiness comes from deeper sources: God, knowing Him, and nurturing relationships with family and friends. These are the real treasures in life that money cannot buy. The relentless pursuit of wealth can distract us from what truly matters.

As an entrepreneur, I understand the drive to make the business successful, aiming to generate more revenue than expenses. However, it's essential to maintain balance and recognize that financial success does not guarantee happiness. Ultimately, joy comes from within, not from material possessions.

To truly grow spiritually, you must spend time with God, read the Bible, and pray. If more people would devote just a small portion of their day to this, particularly first thing in the morning, it would make a significant difference. Getting up just fifteen or twenty minutes earlier can be transformative.

Joining and getting involved in a local, biblically sound church is a powerful way to grow.

PRACTICE SESSION

To turn these ideas into practical tools, use the following prompts and write your definition of success.

Step 1: Measure Success
How do you currently measure each of these: worldly success, business success, and eternal success?

Step 2: Redefine Success
What would success look like if Jesus were your scoreboard? What might you need to release or redefine to live this out?

Reflection Prayer: *Our Father, who art in heaven, please hear my prayer. Let me fix my eyes on eternity and the Word of God to define my meaning of success. The world is so loud, so let me quiet my spirit to hear Your direction and wisdom. In the precious name of Jesus, Amen.*

CONCLUSION

"Seek the kingdom of God above all else and live righteously, and He will give you everything you need."
– Matthew 6:33

I've thoroughly enjoyed watching the U.S. Open tennis tournament, as I am a huge fan of Novak Djokovic. However, I often find it hard to watch the matches live because I get so nervous and tense. To cope, I record the matches and watch them later, knowing the outcome. This approach allows me to feel calm and truly enjoy the experience. Novak Djokovic is a great sports story, but the real significance of this example is that life with faith in Jesus gives us the confidence so that we can win. We are part of a game that has already been won.

By believing in Jesus and following His ways, we can find our purpose. When you align your God-given gifts with His will, you will experience rich, godly success. You can win not only in business but also in the game of life. I invite you to join me in this journey, and I extend this invitation sincerely and from the heart.

I have shared with you my experiences of faith and of God being active in my life.

- Part 1: Who You Are When No One Is Watching

- Part 2: The Big Game: Staying True When the World Pulls Hard
- Part 3: The Victory Walk: Living Like You've Already Won

I have written about seeking God first, aligning your God-given gifts with His will, experiencing rich, godly success (not just worldly success), and winning in both business and life.

I believe with all my heart that God is real, that He loves you, and that He will be there to struggle through life with you. The stories in this book have given you evidence that Matthew 6:33 is true: *"Seek the kingdom of God above all else and live righteously, and He will give you everything you need."* I hope these messages glorify God and transform you.

I have lived through these experiences. I've found some success in business on this side of heaven, and I am confident that I will win in eternal life because I believe I will be living with God in heaven. The key to victory is faith: faith in Jesus, the Son of God who walked this earth and fulfilled the Word. He sacrificed Himself for our sins, rose from the dead, and is now seated at the right hand of our Father.

I have shared my journey with you, but everyone has their own. Faith begins with a step, not perfection. God will meet you where you are. If you repent and choose to follow His path, you will win.

Thank you so much for reading my book. I hope that this message stirs your heart and inspires you to win, fight, and never give up. A significant word here is "fight." I don't mean to associate it with aggression. Instead, I mean to associate it with spiritual perseverance, endurance, courage, and refusing to quit in tough circumstances.

Fighting is something that many people either avoid or hesitate to embrace because it often means struggling. It doesn't always feel good. Fighting requires discipline, obedience, and endurance. It demands a tenacious spirit that refuses to let go or give up. I hope everyone knows they possess more strength and fighting spirit than they realize.

Life is not always pleasant or perfect. We tend to seek ease and comfort, hoping that every day will be a good one. However, that's not how life works. Don't be afraid.

My hope is that my words and stories inspire you to strive for victory and to keep fighting. Don't give up! Knowing you have already won helps keep you targeted on reaching your goals.

Having read this book, you are now on a journey to continue growing spiritually. If you have not stepped out in faith in Jesus, consider saying "yes." If you have stepped out in faith, consider taking the next step in faith, in reflection, or in your church community. Consider working toward deeper discipleship.

Take some time to go back and work through the Practice Sessions in the book. This will give you some clear direction. Life is lived differently when you know you have already won. It is lived with confidence, excitement, and joy. It is a different way to win. Your church is a great resource for opportunities to grow your faith. They can answer questions about your faith or help you get plugged into discipleship groups. For online discipleship, I suggest D-Groups International with Tara-Leigh Cobble.[1]

Thank you again for allowing me to share my stories, and I will keep each of you in my prayers. I don't know all your names, but God does.

---

[1] D-Group International, *Join a D-Group*, D-Group International. https://www.mydgroup.org/joi.

"I press on to reach the end of the race and receive the heavenly prize for which God, through Christ Jesus, is calling us." Philippians 3:14

I'll leave you with this: In "You've Already Won," Shane & Shane sing of a "peace that outlasts darkness" and a hope secured by what "Jesus Christ has won." Even when you're "fighting a battle," you can rest in the truth that He's "already won," so you can "face tomorrow" knowing "tomorrow's in [His] hands" and that "all I need You will provide."

THANK YOU FOR READING MY BOOK!

Just to say thanks for buying and reading my book.
Scan below to access a free, downloadable resource I've created for you.

Scan the QR Code:

I appreciate your interest in my book and value your feedback, as it helps me improve future versions. I would appreciate it if you could leave your invaluable review on Amazon.com with your feedback. Thank you!

www.ingramcontent.com/pod-product-compliance
Lightning Source LLC
LaVergne TN
LVHW010624100826
845148LV00014B/3101

* 9 7 9 8 9 0 1 5 8 1 4 0 7 *